YALE ROMANIC STUDIES: SECOND SERIES

V

Play within a Play

Play within a Play

THE DRAMATIST'S CONCEPTION OF HIS ART:

SHAKESPEARE TO ANOUILH

by Robert J. Nelson

New Haven: Yale University Press, 1958

PARIS: PRESSES UNIVERSITAIRES DE FRANCE

To OLGA

Contents

Preface

As THE MOST objective of literary forms, the drama seems hardly the place for the author to have his say. More than the novelist the playwright is hidden behind his creation; at the furthest remove conceivable from the lyric poet, he has no voice of his own—however numerous his purported surrogates or spokesmen be. For, as recent Molière criticism in particular has made us realize, the spokesman concept can be an especially misleading tool of drama criticism. The very objectivity of the dramatic form should lead us to suspect the notion that any one character is the voice of the author. *His* true voice is the totality of voices which make up his play. In speaking for itself, the play speaks for the author.

In one particular instance, however, the play speaks of itself, offering a double convolution which "shows the seams," turning the dramaturgy inside out. This is in the form of the play within a play, a form which often defines, as it were, the play within which it occurs.

To speak of this unusual configuration is, of course, to evoke *Hamlet*. Shakespeare's most famous work has created the impression in the minds of many that the form is uniquely Shakespearean. The impression is deepened by the fact that the technique or approximations of it occur in a number of his plays: *The Taming of the Shrew, Love's Labour Lost, A Midsummer Night's Dream, The Merry Wives of Windsor, As You Like It, The Tempest*. The fame of what is perhaps the most widely known non-Shakespearean example of the technique, Kyd's *The Spanish Tragedie*, heightens the tendency to think of the structure as uniquely English, if not Shakespearean. Yet it is not English—no more than it is Spanish or French or Italian. Nor is the device peculiar to one historical moment, although certain periods do show an understandable predilection for it. The play within a play is a dramatic technique and it is as such that I examine its use by some of the acknowledged masters of Western drama. I have not attempted to write a history of the device from its origins to its most recent use by Anouilh (a catalogue with plot résumés of plays using it would easily run the length of this book). Rather, I have tried through the study of this index to self-consciousness to isolate a given dramatist's controlling conception of the theater and, secondarily, to trace major movements of Western literature as they have been reflected in the theater. To justify the fact that the majority of my examples come from French dramatic literature, I can do no more than admit to the narrow concerns of the specialist and hope that the reader will find both the examples and the discussion of sufficient interest to excuse my provincialism.

This essay obviously resembles in form and aim Francis Fergusson's penetrating *The Idea of a Theater*. Though I shall disagree with the very "idea of a theater" which Fergusson proposes, I should like to state at the outset my indebtedness to the many insights which make his book a landmark in drama criticism and cultural history.

I shall use a number of terms whose meanings are largely self-evident but which might be made clearer by the following explanations: "primary" or "outer" applied to any traditional term for a play ("action," "illusion," etc.) refers to the play *containing* a play within a play. "Secondary" or "inner" refers, naturally, to the play within a play itself.

I would also add a word on an aspect of the play within a play which I intend to examine only incidentally in this essay: its staging. In a play the written play's the thing. Indeed, when Prospero speaks of the "baseless fabric" of the vision he himself has just evoked, the adjective receives much of its force from the fact that man casts his visions in the ephemeral, intangible forms of language. Of course, a play is more than a string of speeches: the very fact that I propose to examine a particular technique shows my awareness of the play as a *structure*—but this structure emerges through language, that is, as the creation of the dramatist. If battle there must be between dramatist and director (it is more often waged in some critic's mind than in the theater), I am on the side of the dramatist. It is with his conceptions—structural as well as verbal—that I am primarily concerned in this essay.

For readers possibly unfamiliar with the continental plays before Schnitzler's *The Green Cockatoo* I have included résumés in an appendix.

Except where otherwise indicated, I am responsible for all translations from originals. Verse passages have been given in the original as well so that the reader might gain some sense of the poet's language.

Play within a Play is a modified version of a doctoral dissertation done at Columbia University (1955) in which I examined the phenomenon in over one hundred and fifty examples from French literature alone. For much advice on that project I wish to express my thanks to Justin O'Brien of Columbia. To Eric Bentley of Columbia, who served as a member of the dissertation "jury," I owe a debt for the encouragement to revise the original version by extending the inquiry to the drama of other languages. I also share with my contemporaries a more general sense of indebtedness to Professor Bentley, for, in an age dominated by the naive esthetics of "pure art" on the one hand and the simplistic esthetics of *engagement* on the other, his approach to drama as paradoxically pure and *engagé* has set a high example of intelligence and sensitivity. The most deeply felt expression of thanks must go to Henri Peyre of Yale, whose rare tolerance for all points of view held with integrity and coherence has in large measure enabled this book and many others to appear. This tolerance, which does not impair a keen critical judgment, is more than a scholar's passive objectivity; it can be described only by a French word dear to the seventeenth-century French letters he himself has so brilliantly illuminated: *générosité*. The word includes far more than its English cognate, and during my labors of composition that something more has been matched in constancy and intensity only by the faith of my wife, to whom I lovingly dedicate this book.

In that final position which the French reserve for the *mot de valeur* I wish to extend my gratitude to the Ford Foundation for the generous grant which made the publication of *Play within a Play* possible.

R. J. N.

New Haven, Conn.
November 1957

Acknowledgments

PORTIONS of Chapter 3 of this book appeared in *The French Review* of May 1957 under the title "Art and Salvation in Rotrou's *Le Véritable Saint Genest*"; portions of Chapter 4 in *PMLA* of December 1956 under the title "Pierre Corneille's *L'Illusion comique*. The Play as Magic"; portions of Chapter 5 in *French Studies* of October 1957 under the title *"L'Impromptu de Versailles* Reconsidered." I wish to thank the editors of these journals for permission to reprint those portions in this book.

I wish also to make the following acknowledgments in accordance with the wishes of the persons and publishers indicated: to the publishers for permission to use extracts from Jean Anouilh, *Léocadia,* "autorisé par les éditions Calmann-Lévy"; to La Table Ronde for permission to quote from Anouilh's *Colombe, L'Invitation au château,* and *La Répétition, ou L'Amour puni* (in *Pièces brillantes,* November 1951) and *La Valse des toréadors* (February 1952) and *L'Alouette* (November 1953); to E. P. Dutton and Company, Inc., for permission to quote from the editor's translations in *Naked Masks: Five Plays by Luigi Pirandello,* ed. Eric Bentley (Everyman's Library); to the Amministrazione degli Eredi di Luigi Pirandello and to E. P. Dutton and Company, Inc., for permission to use my translation of extracts from *Così è (se vi pare)* and from *Sei personaggi in cerca d'autore;* to the publishers for permission to use my translation of extracts from Sartre's *Kean,* "copyright by Librairie Gallimard, tous droits réservés"; to Criterion Books, Inc., for permission to use my translation of extracts from Sartre's *Qu'est-ce que la littérature?*

It is also a pleasure to record here that my translations of quotations from Luigi Pirandello's *Questa sera si recita a soggetto,* which was copyrighted 1930 by Casa Editrice Mondadori, are used by permission of Marta Abba Millikin, owner of copyright and renewal copyright.

I wish also to thank S. Fischer Verlag, holder of the original copyright, and A. and C. Black, Ltd., holder of the English copyright, for permission to quote from Horace B. Samuel's translation of Schnitzler's *Der grüne Kakadu.*

All literature tends to be concerned with the question of reality—I mean quite simply the old opposition between reality and appearance, between what really is and what merely seems.

LIONEL TRILLING

Chapter 1. The Drama. Ritual or Play?

The play's the thing
Wherein I'll catch the conscience . . .
Hamlet (II.ii)

IN *Our Town* (1938) as earlier in the little-known one acter, *Pullman Car Hiawatha* (published 1931) and later in *The Skin of Our Teeth* (1942), Thornton Wilder has resorted to a dramatic form which expresses his deep hesitancy about just how he expects his audience to take his plays. In presenting them through the frankly theatrical frame of a stage manager (or an announcer in *The Skin of Our Teeth*) who mediates between the audience and the action, Wilder wavers between two opposed conceptions of dramatic art and so leaves us uncommitted to either.

On the one hand, as the Stage Manager talks to the audience about "our" town, they are expected to accept him as a citizen of Grover's Corners, New Hampshire—it is *his* as well as George Gibbs' or Mrs. Webb's town. In fact, at different points in the action, he ceases to be a commentator in order to take a role in the play proper: now as Mrs. Forrest, now as Mr. Morgan, the pharmacist. Thus, in his commentaries, the Stage Manager is not a Stage Manager after all, and what we are looking at in him as in the other citizens is the real thing. The hominess of his commentaries, his vital relationship to his fellow citizens, and his stake in the community's life are intended to obscure for us the otherwise non-naturalistic aspects of the play—the cemetery sequence, for example—and to make us forget that this *is* a play after all. As citizen, the Stage Manager is expected to break down the barrier between stage and audience, to cement in the relationship between the two that total communication—or, perhaps more appropriately, communion—which is said to have characterized the ritual drama of both pagan antiquity and medieval Christendom.

Yet certain aspects of the Stage Manager's role neutralize this

1

ritual view of his behavior. Even before he begins to speak he arranges the scant furniture on the half-lit stage, obviously conducting himself on this very stagy stage not as a citizen of the town but as a member of the troupe putting on the play. In the course of the action, for all his homey remarks to both the audience and his "fellow citizens," he is, through word or deed, constantly shocking the audience out of its acceptance of him as a real person: he is more than just one citizen, the Mr. Morgan we most readily see in him—he is a woman also, the Mrs. Forrest who scolds George for playing baseball on Main Street; again, he manipulates or, in a theatrical sense, directs the various people of the town in their entries and exits; his very first words describing *Our Town* as a play are re-echoed as he cues the audience on the intermissions between the acts; etc. All this restores the invisible barrier between the audience and the stage, interrupts the total communication between the two. It reminds us that the story about the Gibbs is just a play. In fact, it reminds the reflective members of the audience that the Stage Manager in his role as Stage Manager is himself only a character in a play and that the Gibbs' story is actually, if inadvertently, a play within a play.

I say inadvertently, for it is obvious that Wilder does not wish us to take the citizens of the town as actors playing citizens of Grover's Corners. The Stage Manager introduces the "characters" as real people: he tells us that it is Howie Newsome we see delivering milk, not an actor playing Howie Newsome delivering milk. In *Our Town* there is no conflict between the Stage Manager and the actors to provide an outer frame of reference to the essential conflict (what little there is in this lyrical rather than dramatic work). Thus the fashionable Pirandellianism of Wilder's play could not be further from the daring improvisations of the Italian master. Pirandello's "stage managers" in *Sei personaggi in cerca d'autore* and *Questa sera si recita a soggetto* (*Tonight We Improvise*), for all their remarks to the audience, are objectified in their conflict with the actors-as-actors (or as the frankly fictional *personaggi*), a dramatic strategy which, as I shall point out, enables Pirandello to get his "message" home far more tellingly than Wilder's ambiguous use of the Stage Manager. For if the Stage Manager of *Our Town* presents his characters as *real*, he is himself too frequently *unreal* for us to accept his right to do so. As he lets the Stage Manager manipulate the simple folk of Grover's Corners with a wry superiority which puts him above both them and the audience, Wilder takes back, as it were, the message of his play: a comforting reassurance in the homey dignity, the dramatic worthwhileness of the simple life. Hesitating between a ritualistic celebration of the simple life and a straightforward theatricality, *Our Town* forces us to reconsider the very bases of dramatic illusion, to ask: What is a play?

The religious origins of drama have in recent years predisposed many students of the theater to think of dramatic art in varying degrees of identification with ritual. In *The Idea of a Theater,* Francis Fergusson, for example, has developed the anthropological insights of the Cambridge group of scholars to the point of proposing that not only in its origins but in its essence the play is a ritual. To support this view he has depended heavily on the Aristotelian doctrine of mimesis, or on his own gloss on that doctrine: the concept of the histrionic sensibility.[1] Man naturally imitates, says Aristotle. Man naturally dramatizes, reads Fergusson. Now, such a concept buttresses the critic's view of the play as ritual; it concentrates attention on the function and not on the effect of the play. As ritual the actions of the play have a purpose beyond themselves: to celebrate divinity. The actor is not so much actor as priest, the spectator not so much spectator as worshiper.

This approach to the theater poses difficult problems of definition. If the play is essentially as well as historically a ritual, a real action, whence the notion of the play as play, as something which is not "for real?" Part of the difficulty with Fergusson's "idea of a theater" is that it offers, to borrow the critic's own indictment of the modern theater, only "a partial perspective." Fergusson's idea is literally of *a* theater: the tragic theater. To his functional view the critic brings an obvious tragic bias, one which most readily leads him to that ritual which conveys the high seriousness of tragedy: the ritual of the dismembered king or god figure. Yet, logically, there is nothing which precludes Fergusson's idea of the theater as ritual from including comedy. Might not the basis for the comic theater also be ritual: fertility and vegetation rites? The critic is, however, less blind to this conclusion than

might appear: his omission of the idea of a comic theater is consistent with his tragic and realistic bias, for the comic theater is
conventional, unrealistic, and illusory to a much more obvious
degree than the tragic theater.

Nevertheless, tragedy is also conventional, unrealistic, illusory.
A tragedy is a play, not reality itself but an imitation of reality.
Fergusson has betrayed Aristotle's doctrine of imitation by converting it into the doctrine of the histrionic sensibility and by
placing the latter at the service of the reality of ritual. For a play
is not a ritual, though it might, in either its structure or even its
content, imitate one. Fergusson has suppressed the distance between the imitation and the reality it imitates. In doing so the
contemporary critic has been led to falsify the ancient critic even
further. In support of the concept of the histrionic sensibility,
Fergusson quotes Aristotle: "Poetry in general seems to have
sprung from two causes, each of them lying deep in our nature . . . Imitation is one instinct of our nature. Next there is
the instinct for harmony and rhythm." Here is the text in full
from the same translation and the same edition:

> Poetry in general seems to have sprung from two causes,
> each of them lying deep in our nature. First, the instinct
> of imitation is implanted in man from childhood, one dif-
> ference between him and other animals being that he is the
> most imitative of living creatures, and through imitation
> learns his earliest lessons; and no less universal is the pleasure
> felt in things imitated. We have evidence of this in the facts
> of experience. Objects which in themselves we view with
> pain, we delight to contemplate when reproduced with mi-
> nute fidelity: such as the forms of the most ignoble animals
> and dead bodies. The cause of this again is, that to learn
> gives the liveliest pleasure, not only to philosophers but to
> men in general; whose capacity, however, of learning is more
> limited. Thus the reason why men enjoy seeing a likeness is,
> that in contemplating it they find themselves learning or in-
> ferring, and saying perhaps, 'ah, that is he.' For if you happen
> not to have seen the original, the pleasure will be due not
> to the imitation as such, but to the execution, the colour-
> ing, or some such other cause.

> Imitation, then, is one instinct of our nature. Next, there is the instinct for 'harmony' and rhythm, metres being manifestly sections of rhythm.[2]

Through ellipsis Fergusson tends to minimize what in Aristotle seems highly relevant: inseparable from imitation is "the pleasure in things imitated." Indeed, the text has been rendered (by Bywater, for example) [3] so as to make pleasure the second instinct or source for poetry. There is, possibly, some suggestion of an independent esthetic function in that "if you happen not to have seen the original, the pleasure will be due . . . to the execution etc." But unlikely as this may be and although Fergusson's is the more generally accepted rendering on this matter of the two instincts (that for imitation and that for harmony and rhythm), his playing down of the elaboration of pleasure betrays his predominantly ethical and didactic conception of dramatic art. For all his poetic sensitivity, Fergusson, in his largely religious orientation, is primarily concerned not with beauty but with truth. For Aristotle, however, the two are inseparable; poetry for the ancient critic, if not for the modern, is both lesson and leisure, both instruction and delight: "The cause of this again is that to learn gives the liveliest pleasure."

There are, of course, formal characteristics common to both play and ritual: spatial separation from ordinary life, festival atmosphere of mirth and freedom, observance of proprieties, etc. Each activity, as J. Huizinga has seen, transports the participant to another world.[4] But the distinction between the separate worlds of play and ritual is crucial. The supernatural world to which ritual transports the participant has always existed; man discovers it, or, in Platonic terms, rediscovers it. The imagined world to which play transports us, however, is not discovered, but created. To "comprise the sacra in the category of play," believing, as Huizinga does, that "ritual grafts itself upon it, but the primary thing is play" (p. 18)—this is as dubious from the religious point of view as Fergusson's assimilation of play into ritual is from the esthetic point of view. Huizinga is on firmer grounds when he speaks of the "profoundly esthetic quality" of play (p. 2), when he sees that "in this intensity, this absorption, this power of maddening, lies the very essence, the primordial quality of play" (pp. 2–3). For in the *fun* of play "we have to do with an absolute primary category of life, familiar to everybody at a glance right down to the animal level" (p. 33).

A play pleases. A play, in part, is play, action which is self-contained, directed to no end beyond itself, its aim being achieved in its very performance. Play is, so to speak, an Aristotelian first principle, as fundamental as "being" or "doing."

But in a play, it would appear, only the actor plays. Appearances deceive. The spectator plays or "does" (Anglo-Saxon *plegian,* "to exercise, bestir, or busily occupy self") [5] through the mechanism of identification. For the identification to be made, however, the actor must be real to the spectator, the actor in his role must in some way be like the spectator. The mechanism is a function of the reality principle and is the principal mechanism of tragedy. But the spectator plays or "makes believe" with the actor through the complementary mechanism of dissociation: the spectator enjoys the play because it is an illusion. This mechanism is a function of the pleasure principle and is the principal mechanism of comedy. Thus there are two ideas in "the idea of a theater": reality and illusion, or, recalling the etymology of *play,* doing and playing. A play does and does not mean what it says because it is the simultaneous operation of these two ideas. Through this double operation Diderot's famous paradox encompasses not only the actor but also the spectator. It is "le paradoxe du théâtre."

Being an art form, a play is an imitation which pleases. Distinguished from other art forms, a play is a formal imitation of an event through the dialogue and action of impersonated characters. "Formal" is, on the one hand, a key distinction: it is the formality of the structure, of the language, and of the occasion of a play which advises the spectator that he is watching a play. Of these, the indispensable formality is the occasion. (The occasion can, however, be formalized after the fact—as we shall see in Marivaux.) Within it the dramaturgy can differ as much as Racine and Shakespeare differ. Without it there is no play, no imitation, no illusion of reality; there is reality itself. Impersonation, on the other hand, is an equally key distinction. It is true, as a contemporary French philosopher says, that in reality people are persons, while in a play they are personages: "The character of a play lives within the three walls of the setting; the actor as a man watches attentively before the fourth wall, where, in his own way, he finds himself a spectator." [6] But person and personage are as intimately related psychologically as they are etymologically (Latin *persona,* "mask"). For unless the personage *touch* the person, whether that person is the onstage or offstage spectator, the impersonation is without meaning. Formality plus impersonation, then, the one defining the other, are as essential to the play as its event. Impersonation without formality means that the mechanism of identification operates without the mechanism of dissociation—one is fooled. Formality without impersonation means that only the mechanism of dissociation operates— one merely goes "through the forms."

What of the actor for whom the fourth wall is a play? What, in short, is a play within a play? It is a formal imitation of an event through the dialogue and action of impersonated characters occurring within and not suspending the action of just such another imitation. Who defines the inner play as a play? Must it not always be the offstage spectator, the witness of the double action? As we shall see, the formality of the inner action might be presented in such a way (usually for ironic purposes) that, though the offstage spectator has been granted the knowledge, the characters of the containing play might not know that they are watching and, possibly, participating in a false action, that is, a play. Who defines the innerness of the play within a play? Is it not necessarily the offstage spectator, the person in the theater and not the personage on the stage? For the onstage spectator the action of the play within a play is not occurring within some action which he admits to be as unreal as the play he watches. This double relationship, the concept of innerness, obtains only for the offstage spectator.

How old is the formula of the play within a play? Before the play within a play there was, of course, the play within a ritual. The first clearly imitative dramas of the medieval theater are the intercalated tropes of ritual offices. The ritual office is not itself a play. Ritual, like prayer, is a real, not an illusory, action, however dramatic it may be in its effects. Ritual is a mystery, that is, a reality which cannot be explained. Thus the Mass, the most significant ritual of the church, is not an imitation of an action but the mysterious re-enactment of that action. The miracle of transubstantiation of bread into flesh and wine into blood offers not an illusion of reality but reality itself. The frankly impersonated action of the dramatized trope, then, is essentially different from the ritual which suggests it. Dramatized tropes occurring within a ritual, farces intercalated within mystery plays, minstrel *exodia*—such are the medieval formulas anticipating the concentric configuration of the play within a play.

But as long as the play remains connected with the liturgy, its illusory aspect remains only imperfectly defined. The liturgical and semiliturgical drama of the Middle Ages, like medieval painting, is drawn in a single plane of action, in a flat perspective. The simultaneity of décor, "the dramatic principle of the Middle Ages" according to Petit de Julleville,[7] presupposes a two-dimensional perspective. Action is presented in a series of juxtaposed panels as in medieval polyptychs. Whether accidentally or consciously, the artist presents doubleness or even multiplicity of action. The panels of playwright and painter are not behind one another, giving an illusion of depth, but are, in the language of art historians, continuous. A new spatial perspective does not begin to emerge until the theater becomes detached from the church. In the secular theater of the Middle Ages, this new perspective, this doubleness in depth, is anticipated in a number of dramaturgical structures, but it is not clearly defined until the Renaissance. The play within a play is the invention of the modern world.

One might expect to find some significance in the order in which the formula emerges in the principal European literatures, but actually it seems to have arisen spontaneously in each literature. Though Medwall's *Fulgens and Lucres* (1497) is probably the first use of the play within a play,[8] the formula is not peculiarly English. Nor because the formula is here traced primarily in French dramatic literature is there any reason to believe that French dramatists have made the most effective use of it. The significant thing on these questions of chronology is not the order of emergence, nor the distinctions in use, but the common moment of our intellectual history in which this phenomenon emerges. In the Renaissance, the theater is severed from its liturgical context. The concept of illusion generalized at this time derives from the several alternative meanings of *ludo* which the medieval ritual theater denied full importance, but which the medieval secular theater stated with increasing forthrightness as the Middle Ages drew to a close: frolic, dallying, wantonness, mockery, sport, banter, deception, delusion, make-believe, play. For example, the frequent French word for the plot of a play in the sixteenth century, *fable*, underlines the fictional, unreal nature of the dramatic illusion. The view of the play as a *jeu* (Latin *iocus*, whence "joke"), anticipated by Adam de la Halle (*Le Jeu de la feuillée*, 1276), now becomes universal. The didactic principle gives ground before the pleasure principle.

Severed from ritual inspiration, the play loses its all-inclusive character. "To say," writes a renowned medievalist, "that the theater of the Middle Ages lacked that combination of subject-matter and genius which is the formula of a masterpiece is not enough; it seems more just to affirm that the Middle Ages tried a desperate enterprise: to project on the scaffolds of the public square, in the heart of the city and under God's heavens, the work of the creator; but [it must also be affirmed that] this enterprise has left ruins which are still imposing and that it was worthy of the period which conceived and brought to fruit, in the person of the Italian Dante, *The Divine Comedy*." [9] The play, in Francis Fergusson's phrase, is but a fragment of the great mirror it once was.[10] The play is a *pièce de théâtre*, mirroring only a piece or a portion of society, offering only a "partial perspective." The theater no longer contains the world, it is itself contained in the world.[11]

And contained in a very complex world. The Renaissance, as recent cultural historians have taught us, is not single in tone. Theodore Spencer (*Shakespeare and the Nature of Man*) sees it as twofold in expression: affirmation and optimism about man's place in the universe balanced by doubt and pessimism. Wylie Sypher (*Four Stages of Renaissance Style*) views the Renaissance as a sequence of periods of affirmation, disintegration, and re-integration. Yet, whether in affirmation or doubt, Renaissance man views experience in its diversity and multiplicity: "The world," writes Montaigne, "is a perennial seesaw . . . constancy itself is nothing but a still more listless swing." [12] The dualism of appearance and reality, as much as it is seen as a system of analogies and correspondences, is seen as a network of contradictions and deceptions. Appearance belies reality as often as, if not more than, it corresponds to it. The old belief in unity, the old awareness of design, begins to weaken. As the old sense of reality is challenged, not one but several realities clamor for attention. In the clamor it is difficult to distinguish the true from the false, the real from the unreal.

The theater mirrors this dualism of contradictions and deceptions. Disguise themes, magic, dreams, mistaken identities, nocturnal frolics by immaterial dancers—these are the insubstantial substance of the theater of Lope, Calderón, Shakespeare, Corneille, Rotrou, Andreini, Kyd, Molière. It is Roman comedy which the Renaissance, in its attention to ancient drama, most successfully revives, for Roman comedy readily offers this age the image of itself: a world in which things are not what they seem or might not be what they seem. The Menechmi are at home in the Renaissance world.

In a world in which all values are examined, it is inevitable that the instrument of evaluation be itself examined. "Reason offers itself," laments Pascal, "but it is pliable in all directions . . ." [13] Conscious of all doubt, man becomes self-conscious. Not only the meaning of action but the meaning of meaning is examined. The theater mirrors this introversion in that literary form of self-consciousness called the play within a play. The use of this technique implicates within the work of art those considerations which usually remain prior and external to the work. Through the play within a play, Leslie Fiedler has observed, a work offers "a history of itself, a record of the scruples and hesitations of its maker in the course of its making, sometimes even a defense or definition of the kind to which it belongs or the conventions which it respects." [14] The relationship of the inner play to the outer play prefigures the relationship between the outer play and the reality within which it occurs: life. The play within a play is the theater reflecting on itself, on its own paradoxical seeming.[15]

Chapter 2. Shakespeare. The Play as Mirror

> . . . the purpose of playing, whose
> end, at the first and now, was and
> is, to hold, as 'twere, the mirror
> up to nature . . .
>
> *Hamlet* (iii.ii)

I

OF SHAKESPEARE surely we can say what the Danish critic Vedel
has said of Molière: he was truly possessed of the theater.[1] I am
not here subscribing to that false antithesis between playwright
and man of the theater which nonliterary people have in mind
when they use the latter phrase. True, Shakespeare, like Molière,
was a theatrical triple threat: actor-director-playwright. Yet, like
the Frenchman after him, he might have been all these things
and their relevance to his drama been indiscernible to all but the
most knowing of his spectators and readers. We must first trace
the extent of theatrical obsession in Shakespeare where we must
trace it in any dramatist: in the plays as written.

Seven of his plays contain a play within a play or an approximation of the form. However, these inner plays only make explicit
the preoccupation with stage illusion which marks all the plays.
The Shakespearean subplot often serves as a kind of play within
a play, an ironic mirror of the main plot. Whether in the comic
or the tragic mode, all the dramas are "comedies of errors"—
tragedies born of mistaken motives (*Othello, Julius Caesar,* etc.),
comedies based on mistaken identities (*The Comedy of Errors,
The Merry Wives of Windsor,* etc.). Other heroes and heroines
besides Hamlet rehearse their thoughts and deeds before commit-
ting themselves fully. Macbeth and his lady are obvious examples,
but there is, too, young Prince Hal who plays first himself to
Falstaff's mock king, then reverses the roles in order to play king

to the not so mock version of himself given by Falstaff. Spectral creatures as disturbing as the ghost of Hamlet's father haunt and prick the consciences of other Shakespearean characters (in *Cymbeline, Macbeth, Julius Caesar*). Lear deserves censure first of all for the play of emotion he would have his daughters put on; Iago deserves as readily as Hamlet a "fellowship in a cry of players." Finally, the preoccupation with "show, play, and act" which Maynard Mack has found characteristic of the imagery of *Hamlet* marks Shakespearean language in general.[2]

In those plays containing a play within a play, this theatrical self-consciousness becomes explicit. Through this form we can trace the successive stages of Shakespeare's spiritual and artistic development. If we accept the conventional division of the canon into three distinct periods—an early period of affirmation, a middle period of soul-searching, a final period of reaffirmation—we might represent the periods in the following manner: [3]

FIRST PERIOD
The Taming of the Shrew (1594)
Love's Labour Lost (1594)
A Midsummer Night's Dream (1595)
The Merry Wives of Windsor (1599)
As You Like It (1600)

SECOND PERIOD
Hamlet (1601)

THIRD PERIOD
The Tempest (1611)

The plays of the first period show an easy-going, untroubled outlook in the face of the "discrepancy between appearance and reality," which Lionel Trilling has described as the essential theme of all great literature.[4] Reality is given and so, too, is the place of illusion within it. These plays and the plays or masques within them offer themselves as no more than play: actions indulged in for their own sake, preaching no other end than themselves. Like the "sweet comedy" Bottom and his fellows put on in *A Midsummer Night's Dream,* they are the free play of an imagination which has no illusions about the illusions it is creating:

> . . . as imagination bodies forth
> The forms of things unknown, the poet's pen
> Turns them to shapes and gives to airy nothing
> A local habitation and a name.
>   (*A Midsummer Night's Dream*, v.i)

These are plays without epilogues, for the "play needs no excuse" —Theseus's advice to the players at the end of *A Midsummer Night's Dream* being parodoxically reiterated in the epilogue spoken by Rosalind in *As You Like It*. All of the plays I have grouped in the first period are comedies. Here there are no times out of joint, no doubts about one's place and purpose. No star-cross'd lovers those of *A Midsummer Night's Dream* and of *Love's Labour Lost*. With their involved spoofing these plays have a kind of mathematical complexity which looks forward to the manipulations of early Cornelian dramaturgy. The delight one feels in them is as much intellectual as emotional: puzzles are solved, riddles unraveled, wits outwitted by superior wit. This is true even of the fanciful *Midsummer Night's Dream,* where dramatic interest is generated chiefly by the false equations set up by Puck's mismatings.

The head more than the heart is at work. Psychologically, the mechanism of dissociation functions more strongly than that of identification. The onstage spectators of Bottom's "Pyramus and Thisbe" never allow themselves to be committed to or identified with the characters of the play they watch. Their witty, distracting comments define the so-called tragedy as a diversion. The fun-making about the impersonators of the props (Wall, Moonshine) no doubt reflects Shakespeare's self-consciousness about the conventions within which any attempt at theatrical illusion must work, but it does so without that sense of metaphysical anguish we usually associate with the play scene in *Hamlet*. There is perhaps more than a touch of such metaphysical probings in the epilogue, a foreshadowing as it were of the theme of the "insubstantial pageant" so central to *The Tempest:*

> If we shadows have offended,
> Think but this and all is mended—
> That you have but slumb'red here

While these visions did appear.
And this weak and idle theme,
No more yielding but a dream.

Puck's remarks close Bottom's "sweet comedy," but they conclude
Shakespeare's "sweet comedy" as well. Is he not, then, telling the
audience of *Midsummer Night's Dream* (who have already identified themselves with the onstage spectators through their unbe-
lieving attitude to "Pyramus and Thisbe") that they, too, have
"but slumb'red here"? The metaphysical implications are tre-
mendous—the actors-as-spirits of *The Tempest* lie in germ in the
actors-as-shadows of Puck's epilogue. Yet here the probings and
speculations are carried out in the mood of fun which characterizes all the action of the play. As Puck promises to "restore
amends," the dream itself is put into the proper perspective of
the waking world into which the spectators of both inner and
outer play emerge. Ultimately, spectators know themselves for
just that—spectators—whether we speak of those of the play
within a play or those who make up Shakespeare's audience.

As for the actors of the "tragedy," Bottom and his fellows, they
present themselves as no more than actors, and self-admittedly
poor ones at that. They are no more committed to creating an illusion than the spectators are prepared to accept one. The mechanism of dissociation functions smoothly on either side of the curtain, its function being practically guaranteed beforehand in the
social status of actor and spectator: the former belong to the serv-
ing class, the latter to the ruling class. In the class-structured society of Elizabethan England only the most persuasive and sincere
attempts at illusion could allow for identification between lowly
actor and royal spectator. The actor must take his art (if not himself) seriously before the spectator can. Bottom, who is Pyramus,
is not Pyramus but Bottom the weaver and, as Theseus reminds
all at the end of the playlet, "when the players are all dead, there
need none to be blamed." In these early plays, Shakespeare does
not fully ask of us that suspension of disbelief which is an essential
condition of theatrical communion.

The dominant mood here is playfulness. In certain plays this
mood finds formal expression in a stage presentation, in a play
strictly speaking. Yet it does so only under the flimsiest or most

incomplete conditions. In *A Midsummer Night's Dream* the spectators use the pretense of a play as a pretext for their own foolery; the main plot of *The Taming of the Shrew* is, so to speak, a play within half a play, since the induction is never matched by a concluding frame in which we might find a resolution of the playful scheme of the opening frame (we might, for example, expect to find Sly sobered up and disabused). In other plays, however, the playful mood finds little or no formal expression. *Love's Labour Lost* is a game:

> The effect of my intent is to cross theirs
> They do it but in mocking merriment
> And mock for mock is only my intent.
> (Love's Labour Lost, v.ii)

Ferdinand and his fellows would make fun of their ladyloves by playing at Muscovites; but, not to be outwitted, the ladies will fool their lords into making mistaken commitments by exchanging their favors:

> There's no such sport as sport by sport o'er thrown,
> To make theirs ours and ours none but our own:
> So shall we stay, mocking intended game,
> And they well mock'd, depart away with shame.
> (Love's Labour Lost, v.ii)

The game which these royal lovers play sets a tone of mockery and spoofing, one which deformalizes to a large extent the setpiece the ridiculous Armado and the other worthies put on concerning Pompey, Alexander, Hercules, and Judas Maccabaeus. This entertainment is a charade rather than a play, of course, but it has no more chance of succeeding as an impersonation than did Bottom's play. And for the same reason: the spectators, refusing to suspend their disbelief, distract each actor through heckling and catcalls. Moreover, the actors are either too ridiculous (the clown Costard) or of too low station (parish curate, page, pedant) for the spectators to be able to see them in any other way. The French ladies and their retinue are not won over by the entertainment; nor are they presently won over by the protestations of sincerity—exchanged favors notwithstanding—which Ferdinand and his fellow suitors make at the end of the

play. Yet the tone of playfulness remains intact, for, as we have
no doubts at the end of Corneille's *Le Cid* that Chimène will
eventually become reconciled with Rodrigue, so here we have no
doubt that that at the conclusion of the twelvemonth penance
imposed by the ladies, the royal lovers will also be reconciled.
The game has not been played without penalties, but the forfeits
are not enduring.

The set-piece of *The Merry Wives of Windsor* is much more
playlike than either the game which makes up the main intrigue
of *Love's Labour Lost* or the charade in the last act of that play.
The Masque of the Fairies in *The Merry Wives* is not a true
play, of course; it is a stratagem in which there are no spectators,
only actors. The foolers (Falstaff, Slender, Caius, the mother and
father of Ann Page) are fooled by superior foolers (Fenton, Ann
Page, Mistress Ford, Ford, Mistress Quickly). The principal victim of this stratagem is Falstaff, who is thus betrayed in his own
attempts at betrayal. But the intent here is more than mock for
mock: within the terms of the play a very real marriage takes
place and thus frustrates other very real plans for marriage. Ann
Page runs off with Fenton, while Caius and Slender run off with
costumed figures whom they take for Ann but who turn out to be
boys. Of course, Ann Page herself must have been played by a
boy, so that, from the spectator's point of view, Fenton came off
no better than Caius and Slender. Here Shakespeare once again
slyly reminds us of the conventions within which stage illusion is
obliged to function, but he does not allow this self-consciousness
to attain the metaphysical significance it will in *The Tempest*.
Here that the man who makes off with the girl is *really* making
off with a boy remains a joke. If we accept the joke for what it
is worth—that is, if we respect the conventions of the play—we
shall not quibble about who really gets the girl: it is Fenton. And
he has gotten her thanks to a game which turns out to be a little
more practical than the one in *Love's Labour Lost*. If the latter
play anticipates that conception of the theater which prevails in
Marivaux a century and a half later—the play as a game, *The
Merry Wives* anticipates a related conception, favored by many
lesser dramatists of Marivaux's time—the play as stratagem.

As You Like It brings these early plays to a close. Having
donned men's clothing as a stratagem to throw off the duke's

pursuers, Celia and Rosalind finally reveal themselves for the women they really are. Rosalind does so in the playlike pageant in which she is presented by Hymen. As with the Ann Page of *The Merry Wives of Windsor,* the Rosalind who reveals herself to be a woman in this masque was no doubt played by a boy. But here the joke has more point than in the other play. The Ann Page-Slender-Caius-Fenton relationship was really peripheral to the Falstaff-Ford relationship. Fenton's strategic acquisition of Ann was a by-product of the more central stratagem: the upsetting of Falstaff's masked rendezvous with Mistress Ford. But in *As You Like It* Rosalind's self-revelation as a girl is the central issue of the play. If Shakespeare mocked at the conditions of theatrical illusion in *A Midsummer Night's Dream* and treated them as a joke at the end of *The Merry Wives of Windsor,* here his intentions seem a little more serious: no character gets a boy pretending to be a girl (the fate of Slender and Caius in *The Merry Wives*). At the end of *As You Like It* the integrity of the illusion is preserved as the girls playing at boys (the given of the plot), though undoubtedly played by boys (Elizabethan stage conventions), finally reveal themselves as girls. This assertion of the playwright's power over convention, his successful defiance of it, foreshadows the triumph of illusion which marks *The Tempest.* But before the resolutions of that final play Shakespeare will pass through the middle ground of *Hamlet,* in which the most renowned stage director of all dramatic literature combines all the conceptions of the theater we have found in the plays of the early period (diversion, game, stratagem), but adds something more.

II

During the two decades between the First and the Second World Wars, a whole generation saw in the "indecisive" Prince of Denmark the image of itself: it had been done wrong, but could not precisely assign blame. Of all the critical approaches to *Hamlet* those which insisted upon rottenness—both physical and spiritual—prevailed. T. S. Eliot pronounced the play an artistic failure, judging Hamlet (and by implication, the Shakespeare of the *Hamlet* period) more a study for the pathologist than for the literary critic.[5] Hamlet's sense of rottenness, Eliot

maintained in a lapse of moral awareness astonishing for so alert
a Christian moralist, is in excess of the facts as they are presented
to us. Choosing to ignore completely the wicked speed and dex-
terity with which Gertrude posted to incestuous sheets, Eliot con-
veniently found the play without an "objective correlative" to the
"excessive" feeling of Hamlet. The critic's moral lapse was undoubtedly born of an esthetic lapse: the failure to catch the tone
of decadence and corruption communicated by every artistic
means possible in the early parts of the play: the gloomy night
setting of the first scene, the rumors of war, the appearance of
the ghost, the transparently false well-being of Claudius' court,
the presence of the disaffected heir apparent (whatever is wrong
with his psyche), the pervasive imagery of decay balanced by the
equally pervasive imagery of appearances and realities, etc. Eliot's
assessment of the play can be understood historically, of course.
He was writing during a time when "Hamlet and his problems"
(the wry title of Eliot's essay) was the typical approach to the
classic. The approach finally fell into the expert hands Eliot called
for when Ernest Jones psychoanalyzed Hamlet on an imaginary
couch at the remove of three centuries to find in him, to no one's
surprise, a typical case of the Oedipus complex.[6] And in the hands
of less psychologically expert French dramatists, an army of Hamlet types in a spate of bad plays gave voice during the interwar
period to a new *mal du siècle*. In the language of sickness and decay which Caroline Spurgeon found so prevalent in Shakespeare's
play, the very age and body of the time found its "form and pressure." [7]

There has been a healthy reaction to these views in Hamlet
criticism of the past decade. Prompted by Dover Wilson's earlier
What Happens in "Hamlet," imaginative critics like Francis Fergusson, Maynard Mack, Leslie Fiedler, and Robert Speaight have
brought us back to *Hamlet* and *its* problems.[8] Though the movement he sees in the play is centerless, fragmentary, and "toward
chaos," Fergusson's review of the play does study what happens
in *Hamlet* in terms of *action* in the full Aristotelian sense of the
term. And subordinating the role to the play even more, Mack
has subtly observed that paralleling the imagery of disease is an
imagery of action, epitomized in three recurrent notions throughout the play: "show," "play," and "act." Mack has also observed

that one of the very images of sickness which Miss Spurgeon perhaps too hastily assessed as the dominant imagery of the play is *poisoning:* sickness imposed by man in willful act. And Robert Speaight, though retaining many of the bases of Eliot's assessment of the play as an artistic failure, has shown us in the neurotic Hamlet he portrays not a man who acts too little but one who acts too much (an interpretation anticipated in Fergusson's assessment of Hamlet as a grand *improvisateur*). Not why doesn't Hamlet do something about his problems, but why, modern criticism seems to ask, doesn't he stop doing things?

Can we make no sense of the things that Hamlet does?—insult the new king, taunt his faithless mother, deride his mistress, put on a play, slay Polonius, voyage to England, slay his would-be slayers, duel with Laertes, kill Claudius! Are these all the fruits of "an overpowering and immediate emotion [which] put his judgment out of joint" (Speaight)? Is there no pattern to these events?

"Tragedy is essentially an imitation not of persons but of action and life, of happiness and misery. All human happiness or misery takes the form of action; the end for which we live is a certain kind of activity, not a quality. Characters give us qualities, but it is in our actions—what we do—that we are happy or the reverse. In a play accordingly they do not act in order to portray the Characters; they include the characters for the sake of the action. So that it is the action in it, i.e., its Fable or Plot, that is the end and purpose of the tragedy; and the end is everywhere the chief thing." [9] The action of *Hamlet*—what is done—is the effort of a disaffected heir apparent to re-establish order and health to his troubled realm. Now, I do not wish to overemphasize the political in *Hamlet;* I am aware that there is much more to the play than that. Mine is but a minimal definition, a basic statement of what happens, a stone tossed into the surface of the play around which there form the ever expanding circles of meaning I shall examine here.

The basic action pivots around three key events almost mathematically equidistant from each other in the running time (as opposed to the plot time) of the play: the apparition sequence (i.v), the play scene (iii.ii), the dueling scene (v.ii). In each of these

sequences, Hamlet's problem moves one step closer to solution:
What action shall Hamlet take in order to set aright the disordered state of affairs in the kingdom? In each of these crucial
events, the prince illustrates one of the three branches of any act
as they are defined by the gravedigger clown in the burial scene of
the last act: to act, to do, and to perform. Hamlet's *act* after the
apparition sequence consists in *acting*, in putting on an "antic
disposition"; in the play scene, his *act* consists of *doing* something
to make Claudius show his hand; in the dueling scene, Hamlet's
act consists of *performing* (that is, etymologically, of carrying
through to completion) what the ghost has asked of him in the
apparition sequence. Naturally, as events proceed from one to
another, each of Hamlet's *acts* involves all three branches in some
degree. Hamlet's "antic disposition" is a means of *doing* something to forestall any drastic action by Claudius (who might have
a sane Hamlet murdered, as Kittredge points out) [10] and is a first
step in the *performance* of the revenge he must take; Hamlet in-
directly continues his antic disposition as a second stage in the
performance of his revenge in putting on the playlet; finally, in
a profound pun, he "performs" in the duel in order to *do* something about the disordered state of affairs in the kingdom.

   All of these roles are for Hamlet "parts a man might play." In
each of them Hamlet invests the notion of *play* with that connotation of Anglo-Saxon *plegian* which has been increasingly lost since
Shakespeare's time: "to bestir oneself, to do." At any given moment Hamlet shows a fine sense of discrimination as to just what
kind of action is required according to his knowledge of circumstances. We have lived too long with the Hamlet of the suicide
soliloquies. Self-slaughter *is* a possible course of action before
Hamlet's misgivings about his father's death and his mother's
marriage are confirmed through the interview with the ghost.
And, although the more famous contemplation of suicide occurs
after the interview, we have too easily allowed our modern, romantic sense of futility both to exaggerate its importance and,
more seriously, to take it out of its context in the action of the
play. A dramatic soliloquy is a reflection, a state of being prior to
action; its meaning must be assessed only subsequently in terms
of what follows. Dramatically, Hamlet's most famous line reads:
"To be or not to be, that *was* the question." Hamlet rejects

suicide for both moral and psychological reasons: the substance
of the first soliloquy was that the Almighty had set his canons
against self-slaughter; however, Hamlet, being human, has been
tempted to sin against these canons. But he now discovers that
the very nature of the act leaves him no assurance that it will
bring the peace he seeks. So, having rejected suicide, Hamlet
goes on with his antic disposition by berating Ophelia. Is it because he knows (as Dover Wilson has tried to demonstrate in a
close scrutiny of the antecedents of this famous confrontation
scene) that Ophelia has been put to spy on him by him enemies?
At any rate, he now plays the latter off against one another even
more skillfully than he has to date. Thus Hamlet remains as ever
both spectator and performer, an observed observer, as the differing reactions of Claudius and Polonius after the confrontation
testify:

> CLAUDIUS: Love! his affections do not that way tend;
> Nor what he spake, though it lack'd form a little
> Was not like madness.
>
> .   .   .   .
>
> POLONIUS [approving Claudius' plan to dispatch Hamlet to
> England]: It shall do well: but yet I do believe
> The origin and commencement of his grief
> Sprung from neglected love.   (III.i)

Hamlet's antic disposition has served well as a stalling device:
Claudius' temptation to drastic action has been checked; he has
provided a plausible explanation for his "transformation"; he has
begun to unnerve Claudius. Hamlet has been almost completely
convinced privately of the rightness of his suspicions. But his concerns are more than personal; they are public and political, for,
as Prince of Denmark, he has the responsibility to set things
aright. Before he can take any outright political action, however,
he must have "grounds more relative than this." The play's the
thing wherein he'll catch the conscience of the king.

If Claudius but blench at the play, Hamlet shall know that
the ghost is not the devil. This is a lingering doubt in Hamlet's
mind, not a rationalization of his failure to act. The doubt is born
of a very real scruple about the Christian bases of action. As
Dover Wilson has insisted, we must regard the ghost in *Hamlet*

as real. However imperfectly, medieval Catholic theology is still felt as a guide to action in Shakespeare's time. Earlier, Hamlet's first scruple against suicide was theological; later, Hamlet's self-reproaches about his failure to act as he watches Fortinbras cross the Danish plain are theological,

> Sure he that made us with such large discourse,
> Looking before and after, gave us not
> That capability and godlike reason
> To fust in us unus'd.   (IV.iv)

and, ultimately, the bases of the decisive actions of Hamlet in Act v are theological, an echo of the Scriptures: "There's a divinity that shapes our ends" and "There is special providence in the fall of a sparrow." Hamlet is more than a religious man: he is spiritually a sixteenth-century Christian. So here his scruples are theological: ghosts are real, not psychological projections of disturbed mental states; ghosts are either good or bad, angels or devils. In all justice, then, Hamlet cannot act upon the injunctions of a ghost until he is sure that the ghost is angel, not devil. But "The Murder of Gonzago" will settle more than this private doubt. It will justify before the world the revenge Hamlet intends to take upon the murderer of his father. The play within a play is designed to catch more than Claudius' conscience: it must "catch" Hamlet's conscience as well. Conscience for the Prince of Denmark means more than guilt and innocence; it means (as it does in the French language, for example) awareness, consciousness. Morality is a function of perception. Hamlet will not act until the facts are clear and indisputable.

Can a play be described as the means to the revelation of clear and indisputable facts? That school of Hamlet criticism which sees in the young prince only a procrastinator would say no. His play is only another stall: Hamlet would rather rehearse a dead deed than commit a new one and he would rather threaten Claudius with death (in the playlet, we recall, the nephew to the king is the murderer) than actually kill him. Or critics of a more theoretical cast of mind might reply that a play can never be the key to clear and indisputable facts. A play reveals no reality but its own; art and life are distinct and never the twain shall meet. Or to undercut this theory by the ultimate Pirandellian paradox: a play can reveal the one clear and indisputable fact that nothing is clear and indisputable. A whole school of French drama after the First World War took just such a view of Hamlet and of his play. Shakespeare's Hamlet, Jean Sarment (*La Couronne de Carton,* 1920) and his contemporaries felt, put on a play not in order to do something about his problems but simply because he began to doubt their reality. Life is so stagelike, so full of pretense and posture, that a play is not its reflection but its direct expression. In fact, the whole notion of "reflection" meant nothing to the interwar generation bottle-fed on Bergsonism and weaned on Pirandellianism.

But Shakespeare's Hamlet is of another generation. For him, the end of playing, "both at the first and now, was and is, to hold, as 'twere, the mirror up to nature; to show virtue her own feature, scorn her own image, and the very age and body of the time his form and pressure" (III.ii). Hamlet is more than Shakespeare's spokesmen here: he is his own spokesman. His advice to the players bears directly on the uses he puts his play to: it is the image of *his* scorn which Claudius will see in "The Murder of Gonzago," it is the form and pressure of rotten Denmark that the playlet will show. Hamlet, subtle esthetician that he is, knows better than to become immersed in his own art. His advice to the players anticipates the striking proposals of Diderot's first debater in *Le Paradoxe sur le comédien:* "For in the very torrent, tempest, and —as I may say—whirlwind of passion, you must acquire and beget a temperance, that may give it smoothness" (III.ii). "As *I* may say" —for Hamlet himself has had to *play* a role, not live it. Hamlet would not be a "pipe for fortune's finger / To sound what stop she pleases." He would have that man "that is not passion's slave" (III.ii). Such advice is perfectly consistent with Hamlet's earlier reproaches to himself as a "dull and muddy-mettled rascal" upon observing the player who suited his whole function with the forms of his "conceit" (Hecuba's miseries). Hamlet's reproaches to the player were based on the player's lack of smoothness and were fundamentally esthetic in character; his reproaches to himself are based on his strong sense of obligation and are fundamentally ethical.

Hamlet, then, knows the play for what it is: a contest of wits in which he hopes that the esthetically naive Claudius will falter.

Claudius, not his nephew, is the romantic hero of *Hamlet:* whereas
Hamlet's excitement during the play scene is primarily intellectual, Claudius' is primarily emotional. The king is not all un-
controlled feeling, of course. I would agree with those analysts
who insist that the king does witness the dumb show. To have him
distracted (as in the manner of some directors, even the usually
astute Dover Wilson) is to miss the measure of the man. Claudius
steels himself to this first test, this first turn of what Kittredge
calls the thumbscrew. Hamlet has to prick him on with hints and
warnings which become more and more overt as the scene pro-
gresses: "Marry, this is miching mallecho; it means mischief"
(III.ii). Those critics who see Hamlet as angered in these lines
misunderstand the uses to which he puts the dumb show. His
fling at "inexplicable dumb shows" ironically emphasized more the
epithet than the thing. And if, as Leslie Fiedler has said, Hamlet
departs from current stage practices in the very use of a dumb
show,[11] we have all the more reason to interpret Hamlet's comments on it as pointed at the attentive Claudius. But Hamlet is
only teasing and continues to tease with the promise that the
prologue "will tell all." Hamlet's own disappointment in this
prologue ("is this a prologue, or the posy of a ring?") is only
mock, another turn of the screw.

The first scene of the playlet gives the most violent turn of
the screw yet. Claudius remains more or less in control of himself,
but there are signs of his weakening. "Have you heard the argument? Is there no offence in't?" (III.ii). The king addresses the
question more to Gertrude than to Hamlet, thus betraying an
anxiety he expects to find reflected in his wife. But in her he finds
only calm and control. The reasons for this attitude are hard to
assess. Gertrude's protest that "the lady doth protest too much"
seems less brazen when we remember that the Gertrude whom
we have seen in the course of the play has every right to dissociate
herself from the player queen. Never once does she cast a backward glance of remorse or pity for her first husband. True, Hamlet
tells us in his first soliloquy that "she would hang on him / As
if increase of appetite had grown / By what it fed on." Yet this
tends only to confirm our impression of Gertrude as an eroto-
maniac. Still, "she follow'd my poor father's body / Like Niobe,
all tears" (I.ii). The contradiction is only apparent. It is naive to

ascribe moral values to tears. The tears could have been quite genuine, for Gertrude had just been through the great strain of plotting the murder of her first husband and, the deed done, her relief might have expressed itself in tears. However we ultimately assess Gertrude, at this crucial moment she is calm and so restores a measure of calm to her increasingly anxious husband. The latter recovers sufficiently to ask Hamlet the relatively meaningless question: "What do you call the play?" (III.ii). To which Hamlet replies by underlining his true purpose in the least devious of his retorts to date: "The Mousetrap." The king cannot fail to catch the implied threat nor can he fail to sense the implied insult: he, the king, is the mouse, that pesky, essentially insignificant creature which has been scorned by civilized man from time immemorial.

Hamlet's excitement is now itself almost uncontrollable; he has no doubt been encouraged by the evident dismay of Claudius, but he gives the screw one more turn for sure: "This is one Lucianus, nephew to the king" (III.ii). It was not the nephew to the king, of course, who murdered Hamlet's father; but it is the nephew to the king who will murder Claudius. This unmistakable threat must surely rob Claudius of the last shred of doubt concerning Hamlet's purpose. Lest any doubt remain Hamlet explicates the act of poisoning and its consequences in a parallel whose point none present can fail to understand: "You shall see anon how the murderer gets the love of Gonzago's wife."

> OPHELIA: The King rises.
> HAMLET: What, frighted with false fire?
> QUEEN: How fares my lord?
> POLONIUS: Give o'er the play.
> KING: Give me some light. Away!
> ALL: Lights, lights, lights!   (III.ii)

Can we really believe with Speaight that "Claudius rises, *still in command of himself,* and *quietly* asks for lights" (my italics)? [12] Perhaps Hamlet's "frighted with false fire" amounts only to wish fulfillment on the prince's part, but it is absurd not to sense the king's derangement in Gertrude's anxious question and in Polonius' imperious injunction to "give o'er the play." Claudius' own "Away!" hardly bespeaks command and quiet of soul. As that honest witness Horatio has "well perceiv'd," Claudius has blenched. Hamlet has caught a conscience.

The proof has been shown for all to see: Claudius' conduct at the play has settled both the political and the moral questions which earlier stayed Hamlet's hand from decisive action against the king. Politically, Hamlet can now justify overt action against the King he regards a usurper without himself being dubbed usurper; morally, Hamlet can feel that he acts upon the injunctions not of a devil but of an angel. Why, then, does not Hamlet perform the only kind of act called for at this moment of full knowledge: the slaying of Claudius? Of course, he cannot kill the king immediately after the play: Claudius has run to the security of his chambers. But, on his way to his mother's chambers, he has an unparalleled opportunity to slay the slayer of his father as the former kneels to pray. To those who see in Hamlet's hesitancy further evidence of his inability to act, Kittredge suggests that "such an act is not in accord with Hamlet's nature and education . . . Hamlet cannot butcher a defenceless man . . ." [13] So Hamlet has been said to rationalize along the lines of what must be adjudged a twisted theology: Were I to kill Claudius now his soul would go to heaven and my earthly revenge nullified by divine forgiveness. Yet I am not so sure that Hamlet rationalizes here: his religious scruples, a determining factor in his attitude toward the ghost, are very much to the point here as well; he regards himself as the instrument of divine revenge, he is to fulfill the injunction of the angel. Hamlet's theology is undoubtedly all wrong, but it makes him no more inhumane than any of those who subscribed to the code of blood revenge and, at worst, it makes him guilty not of indecisiveness and cowardice but of presumption and pride. Maynard Mack has suggested that before his voyage to England, Hamlet "had been too quick to take the burden of the whole world and its condition upon his limited and finite self. Faced with a task of sufficient difficulty in its own right, he had dilated it into a cosmic problem." [14] With the king, Mack goes on, Hamlet plays at being God. He will act in God's own— that is, *his* own—good time.

That time comes soon. When he believes he has caught Claudius in the unholy act of eavesdropping upon his conversation with Gertrude, Hamlet runs him through. That it is not Claudius

whom he kills through the arras but only Polonius takes no edge
off the decisiveness of Hamlet's act. The act is improvised, but
not impulsive. As earlier with the players, so now with the "hidden
king" Hamlet must make his own occasions for action. That the
justice his act achieves is only poetic is no fault of Hamlet's. Nor
is it any fault of Hamlet's that the occasion for running Claudius
through does not present itself till the moment of the fake duel
with Laertes. Surely Hamlet upbraids himself too much as he
watches Fortinbras' army cross the Danish plain. "How all occasions do inform against me / And spur my dull revenge . . ."
"I do not know / Why yet I live to say 'This thing's to do,' / Since
I have cause, and will, and strength, and means / To do't . . ."
"How stand I then, / That have a father kill'd, a mother stain'd, /
Excitements of my reason and my blood, / And let all sleep . . ."
(iv.iv). These are the reproaches of an impatient man, but not of
one whom we can justly accuse of procrastination. Hamlet has
always taken that action which circumstances and his own knowledge of a given situation have permitted. In this fourth-act speech,
as in his very first soliloquy, he is restive under the rule of a
fate which presents him with no circumstances enabling him to
act upon the knowledge he has acquired. He is, in short, too hard
on himself, for Hamlet is always a man who "had he been put
on / To have prov'd most royally" (v.ii).

It has been through illusion (the apparition sequence) and
pretense (the play within a play) that Hamlet has explored reality,
through them that he moves toward the definitive act by which he
will revenge his father's murder and restore well-being to rotten
Denmark. The real which has given itself as pretense (the "antic
disposition" and "The Murder of Gonzago") has undone the pretense (Claudius' hollow reign and his feighed concern for Hamlet)
which has given itself as real. This fundamental irony of *Hamlet*
is preserved in the final playlike structure of the play, Claudius'
own mousetrap, the fake dueling match of Act v. Once again
Hamlet does something while appearing to do nothing: he turns
the fake into the fatal. But has he not always proceeded in this
manner? The "play" or "show" of action has always had a real
purpose for him. "Hamlet is so much of a professional," writes
Mark Van Doren, "that the man in him is indistinguishable from
the mime. His life as we have it is so naturally and completely a

play that we can almost think of him as his own author, his own
director, and his own protagonist." [15]

This paradoxical equation of the true and the feigned marks
not only Hamlet's but Shakespeare's play as well. Leslie Fiedler
has perceptively observed that by emendation Hamlet does to his
play what Shakespeare did to the *ur-Hamlet*.[16] Shakespeare's play
relates in Hamlet's play its own genesis; Hamlet's "idea of the
theater" constitutes a Shakespearean *art poétique* in miniature.
His conception of the theater in *Hamlet* is far more serious than
that proposed in the earlier plays about playing. There a play was
but "mocking merriment"; here, it is a thing to catch a conscience.
In *Hamlet* Shakespeare moves away from the positivistic separation of art and life implicit in the earlier plays toward an idealistic
correspondence of them. He does not, of course, come to the radical
idealism of a later age for which art and life are one. Art is rather
the mirror of life, and even as we act upon the reflections which
a looking glass gives us (in acts as ordinary as the adjustment of a
tie and as important as the operation of a motor vehicle), so we
can act upon the reflections which art brings us. A play is a long
soliloquy in the several voices which make up our conscience.
It is a state of mind prior to action, the intention which precedes
an effect, the first branch of an act. Art is a reflection upon life
and a reflection of life.

For Francis Fergusson, the mirror of life which Hamlet presents
is fragmented. Such a view is not surprising when we remember
this critic's atomistic and fragmented approach to the play as a
series of "analogous actions" rather than as *an* action. Fergusson
greatly advances Hamlet criticism with his brilliant insights into
the cracked-mirror relationships of stepfather and stepson, false
brother and loyal brother, treacherous wife and trusting husband,
but surely any reasonable reading of the play refutes the critic's
conclusion that the play moves "toward chaos." In addition to his
numerous other parts, Hamlet plays that of a master glazier whose
chief purpose is to repair the fragmented mirrors, that is, to restore to truth the false relationships he finds all about him. If
we are to speak of fragmented mirrors in Shakespeare, it must be
in the early series of plays about the theater. There the mirror
has been fragmented in such a knowing way by a master artificer

that the fragments reflect only each other. In these essentially fantastical plays appearance moves away from reality, appearance is all. Yet we have no lingering doubts that there is a fundamental, stable reality within which the fantasy is delimited. But in *Hamlet* appearance moves toward reality: through pretense we attain the true. At the end of the action, order—political, moral, and esthetic—has been restored. Fortinbras' reassuring arrival and Hamlet's ceremonial funeral are reflections seen in the restored mirror.

Thus Leslie Fiedler's view that *Hamlet* and the play within it embody the myth of cosmic drama seems to me to go too far. "Is not the very piece we are seeing," asks the critic, "precisely that play Hamlet has arranged before us—and are we not then a stage audience, beheld as well as beholding, at a play within some greater play, actors all in a universal drama which inevitably defines all our plays as 'plays within a play?' " [17] Yet if he learns anything, Hamlet learns that all the world is *not* his stage; he learns to limit his ambitions, becoming not an avenging angel but a political assassin (the word need not be taken pejoratively, of course). Though he acts at the behest of the cosmic or the divine, Hamlet leaves ultimate questions, such as Gertrude's judgment, to heaven and seeks only to cure rotten Denmark. He succeeds in this lesser but important mission and so makes whole the reflection which the mirror of the play gives us: that of a fixed, stable social order in which what appears to be so is so.

Hamlet can accomplish this restoration only within the terms of reality as it is given. This is axiomatic of tragedy, of course, and *Hamlet* is a tragedy. The young prince cannot create reality, he can work only on the given. It is easy to understand how this manipulation can lead to the view of Hamlet as either a great *improvisateur* or a compulsive neurotic, but the wonder of his activism is not its improvised character but its usefulness for his major purposes. Even in the play within a play (which Kittredge describes as Hamlet's most decisive action before the actual slaying of Claudius) Hamlet can but insert sixteen lines. Leave it to the Hieronomo of Kyd's *Spanish Tragedie* to merge the real and the unreal and so leave us totally without perspective in a world of chaos. Hamlet is a subtler esthetician and a better metaphysi-

cian. He realizes that his action must be more circumscribed, and
it is this circumscribed action far more than the plethora of
deaths at the conclusion which defines *Hamlet* as a tragedy. The
free manipulation of reality is the essence of comedy and for it we
must look not to the Prince of Denmark but to the lord of the
enchanted isle of *The Tempest*.

III

The central action of *The Tempest* is a "majestic vision" contained between moments of realism and renunciation: the sinking
of the vessel and Prospero's return to Milan. These peripheral
moments are like the frames of the many plays within plays we
have found throughout Shakespeare's theater. And in many ways
the portion contained between these frames itself reminds us of
a play: the isle is the stage; Ariel, Caliban, Miranda, and the
rescued passengers the actors; Prospero that man of the theater
we have recognized Shakespeare himself to have been: playwright,
actor, director.

According to such a view of *The Tempest,* Prospero's pageant
for the betrothed Ferdinand and Miranda becomes a play within
a play within a play. Now, the reflective spectator will regard this
triple convolution—indeed, this logically endless series of convolutions—as implicit in the very use of the technique of the
play within a play. The unwary, looking upon Bottom's "Pyramus
and Thisbe" or Hamlet's "The Murder of Gonzago," cannot believe that those onstage spectators who look at these plays are unreal also, only player kings and player queens. But the more reflective will sense with Fiedler the implications of the double
convolution: if the players are but looking at a play, what are
we doing but looking at a play, and is there some still more
ultimate audience looking upon us and itself being looked upon,
ad infinitum? The world-stage concept is the very essence of the
play-within-a-play idea. Yet, as we have seen, from the *Taming of
the Shrew* through *Hamlet* Shakespeare has tried by various means
to delimit the series of convolutions: to the extent that the wary
spectator does identify with the onstage spectator in the early
series of plays about the theater, Shakespeare tells them to take

his play no more seriously than Theseus and his fellow nobles take the "sweet comedy" offered by Bottom and his fellows; in the very contrast which he presents between the esthetically aware Hamlet and the esthetically naive Claudius, Shakespeare warns us not to take the play we are looking at so unreservedly as Claudius, but, rather, to identify with Hamlet who knows to just what uses a play may and may not be put. In *Hamlet,* as in the earlier plays, the planes of reality and illusion remain separate and distinct—at least for those spectators who do not seek to be confused.

But in the central action of *The Tempest,* the various planes of action dissolve. The action of the pageant and that of the primary intrigue occur within a single plane: the actors of the play within a play are not professionals to whom we can attribute a real life beyond the confines of the illusion in which they appear. They are as real or as unreal as the spectators before whom they parade. Indeed, they are not actors but

> Spirits, which my mine art
> I have from their confines call'd to enact
> My present fancies.   (IV.i)

And so too are spirits those "actors" who follow Prospero's directions in the specifically nontheatrical events of the main action: Ariel, who is not only Prospero's stage manager for the pageant but who also creates the tempest itself and guides at Prospero's behest the destinies of its victims; and Caliban, the evil spirit who bends to Prospero's directions only with the greatest ill will. And are not Ferdinand and all who are saved from drowning by Prospero's art themselves spirits, living beyond the death we surely assign them to after the loss of their vessel? Finally, are not Prospero himself and Miranda like spirits, living in a magical world, an enchanted isle suspended between the physical realities of Naples and Milan and between the temporal realities of Prospero's usurped reign in the long ago of Milan and the contemplative future to which he makes his return at the end of the play? "A spirit" Miranda calls Ferdinand when asked by her father to identify him when first she sees him—"a thing divine for no thing natural. I ever saw so noble" (I.ii). "Goddess" Ferdi-

nand in turn addresses Miranda, divine and miraculous not only
in her very name but in the innocence and purity of which her
virginity is the shining example.

Thus the most pervasive image pattern of the play evolves
around the single word "spirit." In a spirit appearance and reality
coincide by definition; appearance is reality. This we have already observed of Miranda, but is it not true as well of all the
personages of the play?—the noble Ferdinand, who proves by his
actions the nobility Miranda immediately ascribes to his form;
Caliban, in whom not only the very ugliness of his form but the
very harshness of his language corresponds to his baseness; the
major usurpers Sebastian and Antonio, who openly avow their
conscienceless ambition; the minor usurpers Trinculo and
Stephano, whose base natures lead them into league with the base
Caliban and whose depravity is represented in their drunkenness?
The *drama* of the play is a contest between spirits: Shakespeare
has schematically arranged these spirits in a hierarchy ranging
from the evil to the good and at each level has pitted forces of
good against the forces of evil: Ariel-Caliban, Alonso-Sebastian,
Prospero-Antonio. But in these struggles Prospero's role is more
than that of usurped ruler seeking restoration of his domain. He
is playwright and director as he abets the efforts of the good
spirits and impedes those of the evil. But where Hamlet was forced
to improvise, that is, to work his will only within the circumstances imposed by fate, Prospero freely creates his own circumstances, is master of his own fate.

The primary mode of *The Tempest* is comic and its major
theme freedom. As Prospero works his will, we are made aware
not of man's limitations but of his possibilities. The crucial representation of these possibilities is symbolically offered in the play
within a play strictly speaking, the pageant put on before the
betrothed couple. The very occasion expresses the theme: the
wedding engagement of two perfect and perfectly matched people before whom lies a new, rich life. The content of the pageant
reinforces this vision of promise and fruitfulness: Juno, mother
goddess of the heavens, and Ceres, mother goddess of earth, celebrate in song the rich life lying before the lovers; Iris and the
nymphs celebrate it in dance, joined by the reapers, those bring-
ers of abundance. And reigning over all life-bringing spirits is

Prospero, godlike in his power, himself an overwhelming figure of fecundity and freedom.

But Prospero "starts suddenly" and dispels these blissful spirits, for he has remembered the blighting spirit of Caliban:

> You do look, my son, in a mov'd sort,
> As if you were dismay'd: be cheerful, sir:
> Our revels now are ended. These our actors,
> As I foretold you, were all spirits and
> Are melted into air, into thin air:
> And, like the baseless fabric of this vision,
> The cloud-capp'd towers, the gorgeous palaces,
> The solemn temples, the great globe itself,
> Yea, all which it inherit, shall dissolve
> And, like the insubstantial pageant faded,
> Leave not a rack behind. We are such stuff
> As dreams are made on, and our little life
> Is rounded with a sleep.—Sir, I am vex'd:
> Bear with my weakness; my old brain is troubled.
>
> (IV.i)

From this point on the mood of *The Tempest,* the epilogue apart, turns melancholy, if not somber. Henceforth Prospero uses his arts not to celebrate life but to administer justice. Ultimately, in fact, he renounces his arts, and this famous "revels speech" anticipates that renunciation in the last scene of the play. In the revels speech the world-stage metaphor paradoxically becomes explicit in the convolutions it had previously implied, but the only way in which Shakespeare seems to be able to escape the infinite series of play within a play within a play within a play is by an act of dissolution. The triumph of illusion has been but short-lived. Between the revels speech and the epilogue, the mood of *The Tempest* shifts from the comic to the tragic or something akin to it. As in tragedy, Prospero ultimately recognizes a limit to man's possibilities. He leaves his enchanted isles and abandons the untrammeled exercise of his seemingly limitless powers in order to return to Milan "where / Every third thought shall be my grave" (v.i). Thus not life but death—that inescapable limitation upon life and its possibilities—is the last concern of Prospero within the play proper. Shakespeare here seems to be sadly reiterating to himself a doubt in the value of the "baseless fabric" of his own vision, the plays which he has spent a lifetime in creating. There seems even to be a more profound disillusionment with all the world and man's place in it as Prospero consigns to dissolution "the great globe itself."

But "be cheerful, sir," Prospero advises Ferdinand even before he consigns all to this dissolution. Yet the bases for cheer do not become clear until the epilogue of the play:

> Now my charms are all o'erthrown
> And what strength I have's mine own;
> Which is most faint: now, 'tis true,
> I must be here confin'd by you,
> Or sent to Naples. Let me not,
> Since I have my dukedom got
> And pardon'd the deceiver, dwell
> In this bare island by your spell;
> But release me from my bands
> With the help of your good hands.
> Gentle breath of yours my sails
> Must fill, or else my project fails,
> Which was to please. Now I want
> Spirits to enforce, art to enchant;
> And my ending is despair,
> Unless I be reliev'd by prayer,
> Which pierces so that it assaults
> Mercy itelf and frees all faults.
> As you from crimes would pardon'd be,
> Let your indulgence set me free.

Technically an epilogue is superfluous, not an integral part of a work, and customarily the actor who speaks the epilogue of *The Tempest* steps out of the character of Prospero. But who would play *The Tempest* without its epilogue and who but Prospero would recite it? For it is to Prospero and not to the actor that these lines belong. In them he reasserts his confidence in life's possibilities—those not of a life "rounded" with death but of a life without end. The epilogue re-establishes the comic mode without blinking the fact of death and of man's earthly limitations, for death is transcended in the Christian promise of another life.

The various conceptions of the theater which Shakepeare has heretofore entertained (diversion, stratagem, maze, mirror) give way before the ultimate metaphor, that of the divine comedy. The gorgeous palaces of his theater as well as the great globe itself, Shakespeare finally tells us, dissolve not into the nothingness of death but into the everlasting glory of God.

It would be idle to deny that the Christian resolution of *The Tempest* involves the "dissolution of the great globe itself." Prospero, if not Shakespeare, turns his back upon his magical arts; he gives up *his* theater. Since the play never becomes specifically theological, it is difficult to assign sure doctrinal reasons for this renunciation. Whether Shakespeare was a Catholic or a Protestant is as meaningless a question as whether he was really someone else. However, we can say that there is something Calvinistic (and there are Calvinistic Catholics) in that implicit denial of the esthetic in the name of the ethical which the conclusion of *The Tempest* offers. Without condemning the esthetic, *The Tempest* is one of the first plays to take a stand, however guardedly, on the struggle between the ethical and the esthetic which marks much of the theater about the theater in the seventeenth century. Let us turn to this struggle as it is waged by three of the greatest French dramatists of the period: Rotrou, Corneille, and Molière.

Chapter 3. Rotrou. The Play as Miracle

> And my ending is despair,
> Unless I be reliev'd by prayer . . .
> *The Tempest* (Epilogue)

MANY are beginning to consider Jean Rotrou (1609–50) a worthy companion for the great three of seventeenth-century French dramatic literature: Corneille, Molière, and Racine. He is the author of some thirty plays, the majority tragicomedies, the prevailing form of the tempestuous period in which he wrote. The violence and scope of his conceptions make one think of Elizabethan revenge tragedy, and his *Venceslas* (1647), in particular, is a bloody piece in the best Marlovian tradition. Murder, lust, treachery, ambition are favorite themes of his work, and since they are often expressed in an elegant, "conceited" style, the resulting tension of form and content has led some critics to describe his drama as baroque. Certainly, as in much baroque art, the stark contradiction of appearance and reality is a constant problem confronting his characters. Indeed, this contradiction extends to the man himself, for behind the appearance of the bloody plays lay the reality of the deeply religious man. It is not surprising, then, that in *Le Véritable Saint Genest* (1645) the subject of the actor who becomes converted through his acting should prove doubly irresistible to him as both practicing dramatist and practicing Catholic.

Religious drama reached a peak in the middle years of the seventeenth century in France. Corneille had turned to the subject of martyrdom and conversion in *Polyeucte* (1640) and the story of Genest had already served as the subject of Desfontaine's *L'Illustre Comédien* the year before Rotrou turned to it. It is evident, however, that neither Corneille nor Desfontaines had so great an influence upon Rotrou's play as Lope de Vega, from whose *Lo Fingido Verdadero* (1600?) Rotrou took the general plan of his own drama, and Louis Cellot, from whose Latin drama

Sanctus Adrianus, Martyr (published 1630) he took the substance of his play within a play. Even here, however, what stands out is not the influence but the difference between the play and its sources. Lope's tale of the actor converted is a sprawling canvas in which the first act is devoted to the story of Diocleciano's rise to emperor. Lope's play contains two inner plays, one in which Ginés acts the role of a jealous lover and the other that of a converted Christian. Significantly, in neither of these is Ginés ever very far from his true feelings: in the first play he gives vent to the real jealousy occasioned by his love for the actress Marcela, who loves another actor, Ottavio; in the role of the convert, Ginés acts almost not at all, for he is no sooner onstage than he professes *his*—not the role's—new-found faith. Lope thus never maintains that doubleness of perspective which defines both the paradoxical dramaturgy and the paradoxical theology of Rotrou's play. As in much "official" religious art, the Spaniard is too literal, too obviously programmatic and, even if we must ultimately assess Rotrou's intentions as equally programmatic, we shall have to acknowledge nonetheless that his dramaturgy is more skillful and his theology more subtle.

The play about Adrien, the trusted officer of Maximin's retinue who was converted while carrying out a persecution against the Christians, is to be presented as a diversion for the coemperors Maximin and Dioclétien. During these scenes which occur before the appearance of Genest, Dioclétien, the foot soldier become emperor, provides in his own career an ironic parallel with that of the actor:

> Et moi-même, enfin, moi, qui de naissance obscure,
> Dois mon sceptre à moi-même et rien à la nature,
> N'ai-je pas lieu de croire, en cet illustre rang,
> Le mérite dans l'homme et non pas dans le rang,
> D'avoir à qui l'accroît fait part de ma puissance,
> Et choisi la personne et non pas la naissance. (I.iii)

> (And I, of obscure birth, I who owe my scepter to myself and nothing to nature, have I not reason to believe, from this illustrious rank, that merit lies in the man and not in the rank, have I not had reason to give part of my power to him who increased it, to have chosen the man and not his birth?)

From lowly foot soldier to emperor—even as Genest will pass
from lowly actor to saint. Of course, before becoming a saint,
Genest himself sycophantically shares the world values of the emperors. The Genest who discusses with the emperor the virtues
of various plays is clearly pagan, a professional actor seeking only
a chance to please, a Genest for whom the playing of a Christian
martyr is nothing more than a play. Agreeing to present a play
about the martyr Adrien for which he has already gained some
fame, the actor tells the court:

> Elle sera sans peine
> Si votre nom, Seigneur, nous est libre en la scène
> Et la mort d'Adrien, l'un de ces obstinés,
> Par vos derniers arrêts naguère condamneés
> Vous sera figuré avec un art extrême,
> Et si peu différent de la vérité même,
> Que vous avoûrez de cette liberté
> Où César à César sera représenté,
> Et que vous douterez si, dans Nicomédie,
> Vous verrez l'effet même ou bien la comédie. (I.v)

(It will be without difficulty, my lord, if your name is at
our disposition in the play. The death of Adrien, one of these
obstinate believers, will be shown to you with extreme art,
so little different from truth that you will allow this liberty
whereby Caesar will be shown to Caesar; and you will wonder if, in Nicomedia, you are seeing the thing itself or indeed
a play.)

Even when he presents the play within a play front and center,
so to speak, Rotrou never lets his spectator forget the structural irony of the conversion within the diversion. The peripheral
scenes of each act of *Le Véritable Saint Genest* revert to the onstage spectators or else to the actors of the "Martyrdom" in their
offstage roles; the inner play begins in Act II only after a long
series of scenes backstage where we see Genest try to persuade
the actress Marcelle, who is to be his onstage wife, to put real
feeling into her role; and still in Act II just before Genest goes
onstage he has a premonition about the true meaning of the
words he is to speak only in derision; at the end of Act III the

spectators hasten backstage to congratulate him on the force of his performance; Act III begins with the spectators discussing the performance and ends with Genest breaking out of character in order to complain about a noisy crowd which disturbs the performance; Act IV begins with the announcement that the disturbance has been quelled and it is in this fourth act of the over-all play that the inner play comes to an end with the actor's conversion. Finally there is a long fifth act in which the spotlight falls exclusively on the members of the court. The entire play is a constant, skillful shifting from one plane of action to the other, from one scale of values to the other.

Details of language enforce this structural contrast between the worldly court and the otherworldly subject of the play given before it. "En cet acte," Dioclétien tells Maximin at the end of Act II, "Genest à mon gré se surpasse" (II.ix). The key words here are rich in double meaning: "acte" is at once a theatrical and religious term (for example, *Actes des Apôtres*), and though it is surely only the profane sense which the emperor intends, the spectator of Rotrou's play cannot fail to grasp the irony involved. Again, Genest is surely surpassing himself onstage in a double sense: both as actor and as person, for, troubled by the lines he says as Adrien, he is passing beyond his old self into a newer self. And Rotrou seems to underline the religious sense of the emperor's words, when Maximin replies: "Il ne se peut rien feindre avecque plus de grâce" (II.ix). "Grâce" could not be more ironic on the lips of this persecutor of the Christian, for it is indeed Christian grace which is enabling the actor to surpass himself in this act.

Naturally, the contradiction between appearance and reality is brought out most strongly in the playing of the "Martyrdom of Adrien." Genest reacts to this role in a way that the other actors do not. Marcelle, for example, who is to play Genest's wife Natalie, cannot understand Genest's exhortation that she try to bring greater feeling to the role of the Christian wife. But, unlike Diderot's unmoved actor, Marcelle is openly hostile to the sentiments of Natalie, so much so in fact that she feels incapable of playing the role well. Little more than a coquette, she cannot in her simple materialism "rendre touchante une femme crédule/ Qui mieux qu'un bel époux préfère un sot trépas" (II.iii). (". . . render touching a credulous woman, who, instead of her

handsome husband, prefers a stupid death.") When Genest appeals
to her in the name of a subtle esthetic of acting-by-analogy from
her personal experience, her essentially antiparadoxical spirit prevents her from meeting him more than halfway: granted that she
might even have been willing to have suffered death for a cher-
ished object, "Certes je n'aurois pas au milieu des supplices/
Savouré les douleurs comme autant de délices" (II.iii). ("Certainly,
in the midst of torture I would not have savored my pains like so
many dumb delights.") When Genest persists in his appeals, Marcelle warns him against running the risk of attributing any greatness of soul to the Christians; she shrewdly observes that the
Christian blood which the emperor has made flow has already
brought them too much honor. In defending the pagan and
worldly values of her masters, the actress states one side of the
debate which will henceforth trouble the acting of Genest.[1] The
other side is heard in the voice of the angel telling Genest that he
will not imitate in vain, that "Ton salut ne dépend que d'un peu
de courage,/ Et Dieu t'y prêtera le main" (II.iv). ("Your salvation
depends upon only a little courage, And God will lend you a
hand in it.")

"The Martyrdom of Adrien" continues the debate: the Christian side is heard in the words of Adrien, Natalie, and their
mentor, the aged Anthime, while the pagan side is heard in the
onstage Maximin and the Roman officer, Flavie. Nineteenth-
century critics especially objected both to this doubling of the
action and to the extreme length of the play within a play.[2] However, far from the canons of the well-made play and imbued with
Pirandellian notions of intertwined actions, we can appreciate the
great skill of Rotrou's dramaturgy in this connection. By reaching
back into the main plot for the source of his secondary plot,
Rotrou not only maintains a thread between the two but also
maintains the forward motion of the first. As Genest in the role
of Adrien listens to the reproaches of Flavie and the impersonated
Maximin, he hears the charges of ingratitude and disloyalty which
the offstage Maximin would surely address to him, should he,
like Adrien, renounce the Roman gods. Genest's relationship to
the emperors parallels exactly Adrien's before his conversion: that
of a trusted servant who deals with the Christians only for the
purpose of enforcing the emperor's anti-Christian policies. The
play within a play, constructed as a flash back, thus remains

present and moving, and logically continues the action of the offstage events.

The intensity with which he listens to this debate accounts for the extraordinary force of Genest's acting: "Dedans cette action, [Genest] passe aux derniers efforts de sa profession" (IV.i). The debate ends when Genest renounces the profession of acting for a profession of faith. The attentive spectator catches the moment of conversion even before Genest explicitly announces it— at that moment when Genest as Adrien, seemingly still in character, turns to the aged Lentule who plays Anthime, and addresses his fellow player by his offstage name:

> Ha! Lentule! en l'ardeur dont mon âme est pressée,
> Il faut lever le masque et t'ouvrir ma pensée: (IV.v)

(Ah! Lentulus! in the ardor which seizes my soul, I must doff the mask and open my mind to you.)

Filled with his new faith, Genest declares it openly:

> Adrien a parlé, Genest parle à son tour.
> Ce n'est plus Adrien, c'est Genest qui respire
> La grâce du baptême et l'honneur du martyre; (IV.v)

(Adrien has spoken, Genest speaks in his turn. It is no longer Adrien, it is Genest who breathes in the grace of baptism and the honor of martyrdom.)

There is no longer any need of a play manuscript, Genest tells his discountenanced fellow players. In the play in which he is now acting, he continues, an angel holds the script and

> Ce monde périssable et sa gloire frivole
> Est une comédie où j'ignorais mon rôle.
> J'ignorais de quel feu mon coeur devait brûler;
> Le démon me dictait quand Dieu voulait parler;
> Mais, depuis que le soin d'un esprit angélique
> Me conduit, me redresse et m'apprend ma réplique,
> J'ai corrigé mon rôle, et le démon confus,
> M'en voyant mieux instruit, ne me suggère plus.
> J'ai pleuré mes péchés, le Ciel a vu mes larmes;
> Dedans cette action il a trouvé des charmes,
> M'a départi sa grâce, est mon approbateur
> Me propose des prix, et m'a fait son acteur. (IV.vii)

(This perishable world and its frivolous glory is a play in which I ignored my role. I did not know with what fire my heart was to burn; the devil prompted me when God wanted to speak; but ever since the care of an angelic spirit leads me on, corrects me, and teaches me my replies, I have corrected my role, and the devil, confused, seeing me better instructed, no longer prompts me. I have lamented my sins, heaven has seen my tears; in this action, it has found a certain charm, has granted me grace, has approved me, offered me prizes, has made me its actor.)

The professional actor uses theater language in order to explain what has happened to him: life is a stage, God and the devil rival prompters, the play's rewards are prizes, etc. By dint of his conversion, Genest restores much of the original meaning to this figurative language: "Dedans cette action . . . le Ciel . . . m'a fait son acteur." *This action* is a real action, activity and not pretense; Genest is here a true actor—a doer, not a pretender. But the effect of this language can only be puzzling to the ears of the unconverted fellow actors and spectators of the court play. Realizing this, Genest must underline the literal sense of his stage language in order to convince his hearers that his conversion has been a real one:

> Ce n'est plus Adrien, c'est Genest qui s'exprime;
> Ce jeu n'est plus un jeu, mais une vérité
> Où par mon action je suis représenté,
> Où moi-même, l'objet et l'acteur de moi-même
> Purgé de mes forfaits par l'eau du saint baptême,
> Qu'une céleste main m'a daigné conférer,
> Je professe une loi que je dois déclarer.   (iv.vii)

(It is no longer Adrien, it is Genest who speaks; this game is no longer a game, but a truth wherein I am represented by my own action, wherein I, the subject and the actor of my part, purged of my crimes by the waters of holy baptism which a heavenly hand had deigned to confer upon me, profess a law which I must declare.)

The "profession" of Genest is no longer esthetic, but religious. The disturbance in his breast, kindled by the mysterious voice of

the angel, has come to an end. The student of the Renaissance or
the reader of Shakespeare discovers in the language of the converted actor familiar themes. As with Hamlet, so with Genest: a
play has confirmed an insight into reality; through pretense the
hero has found a basis for meaningful action, where before all
had been meaningless. The play has been a thing with which to
catch a conscience, a Shakespearean notion particularly apt for
the religious outcome of Genest's play. Still more, "all the world's
a stage"—yet Rotrou's actor invests this Shakespearean notion
with a literalness which marks a return to Dante's conception of
life as a great play of which God is the author, man the actor, the
cosmos the stage, eternity the duration, and salvation versus
damnation the theme. The mortal phase of human life makes up
but one act of this divine comedy, a fact which explains Rotrou's
continuation of the play not only after Genest's conversion but
also after his martyrdom. A century ago, Sainte-Beuve complained
that Rotrou missed a fitting climax to his play by showing the
other actors and the royal spectators apparently unmoved by
Genest's conversion; remembering the plethora of conversions at
the end of Corneille's *Polyeucte,* the critic would have Rotrou
convert everyone else in his play as well.[3] Yet Rotrou would only
have sacrificed the essential irony of his play: that the others should
be unimpressed by the conversion of the actor gives point to that
conversion. Untouched by the gift of divine grace, the actors and
courtiers remain committed to worldly values.

Through his own conversion, Genest rejects such values completely. One implication of his new-found faith is, obviously, that
he must no longer play saints in derision. But more drastically
still, there is the implication that he must no longer play at all—
even in praise of saints. The actor must give up the theater:

> Il est temps maintenant de réjouir les anges,
> Il est temps de prétendre à des prix immortels,
> Il est temps de passer du théâtre aux autels.   (iv.vii)

> (It is time now to make the angels rejoice, time to aspire to
> immortal prizes, time to pass from the stage to the altar.)

The worldly theater is a fiction, a make-believe, a lie. Though
perhaps not sinful in themselves, the plays of that theater distract
us from taking a full and serious part in the infinitely more im-

portant play whose rewards are not ephemeral applause and mortal happiness but eternal salvation and everlasting glory. The esthetic of *Le Véritable Saint* Genest is antiesthetic. According to the insights of his own actor, Rotrou should not have dallied with *Les Sosies, Amélie,* or any of his earlier plays. For these past "sins" the playwright can be forgiven, naturally, if the insights of *Saint Genest* were not gained until the moment of that play's composition. Then, however, Rotrou should not have continued to write such worldly plays as *Venceslas* (1647) or *Cosroès* (1648). Perhaps even, in view of the antiesthetic of *Saint Genest,* the playwright should not have written *Saint Genest* itself. This paradox reminds modern readers of Paul Valéry's conviction at one stage of his poetic development that the artist should not create works of art, for the commitment to paper inevitably involves esthetic loss. In Rotrou's case, however, the paradox has a theological basis: if *Le Véritable Saint Genest* has been offered only to please, if like the "Martyrdom of Adrien" it is a mere *divertissement,* then Rotrou should also heed the reproaches Genest addresses to himself for having "acted" only in mockery before his conversion.

Yet the view of the theater suggested by Rotrou's play can be reconciled to the *fact* of the play, that is, to Rotrou's having written it at all. The solution lies in a consideration of the inspiration rather than of the form of the play. For if the form of *Le Véritable Saint Genest* is that of French classical tragedy, its inspiration lies in the religious theater of the Middle Ages, specifically in the *miracles* and *mystères:* the dramatized saints' lives of the thirteenth and fourteenth centuries. A noted student of French religious drama of the seventeenth century has written: "Grace and miracle are not synonyms. The miracle is the soul of medieval drama; it is the material form of grace . . . by its miracles *Saint Genest* is a mystery play." [4] In this play about an actor converted while acting, Rotrou implicitly rejects the conception of the play as a mere diversion and returns to the dying conception of the play as a ritual. When Genest announces that "it is time to pass from the stage to the altar," Rotrou has in effect converted his stage into an altar. Like his medieval predecessors the playwright has provided an occasion for the grace of God to work its ways among men's souls. At the very least, Rotrou's play shall be the celebration of the twin mysteries of divine grace and human freedom; at the most, the play shall be the instrument of conversion either for the actors or the spectators. To suggest, however, that the play is only a play, a paradox conceived to astound and amuse, is sacrilegious. It implies that there is something more important than the miracle of the ritual play. We can appreciate even better in the light of this interpretation the sound (for him) doctrine as well as the sound dramaturgy which led Rotrou to refuse to follow Corneille's *Polyeucte* by converting everyone in sight at the end of the action. The emperors, the courtiers, and the other actors remain unconverted as an illustration of the orthodox Catholic doctrine that "many are called, but not all agree to be chosen." The spectators of "The Martyrdom of Adrien" mirror the spectators of Rotrou's own play: they are divided into those who respond to the miraculous message of the play and those who do not, into the Genests and the Maximins.

Rotrou's play thus presents an accurate image of that seventeenth-century world in which the secular uses of the theater begin to overwhelm the more traditional ritual uses. *Saint Genest* is half miracle, half diversion; half ritual, half play. Having written *Saint Genest*, Rotrou continued to write not miracle plays, as the esthetic of *Saint Genest* clearly demanded of him, but quite simple plays. He heeded not Genest, but Maximin. As in the Corneille to whom he is often compared there is in Rotrou a fissure in reality: between the ethical and the esthetic, between the real and the apparent. In rejecting the illusoriness of art through the lesson of Genest, Rotrou rejects the very form in which the lesson is presented to us: a play, which is a work of art. Art is illusion and to cultivate the illusory, Genest teaches us, is sinful. Rotrou, of course, seems as little bothered by this contradiction as that other great Catholic dramatist, Calderón, whose Segismundo also prepares for the world of eternal reality by action in the world of appearance:

> A reinar, fortuna, vamos
> No me despiertes, si duermo.
> Y si es verdad, no me aduermas.
> Mas, sea verdad ó sueno,

Obrar bien es lo que importa;
Si fuere verdad, por serlo;
Si no, por ganar amigos
Para cuando despertemos. (iii.iv)

(O Fortune, let us go reign. Do not awaken me if I sleep and
if it is true don't put me to sleep. But if it be truth or dream,
what counts is to do the right thing. If it be true, then for
that alone. If not, in order to win friends for when we
awaken.)

For in the marriage of art and morality or of human freedom and
divine grace forged by the Catholic apologists of the Counter
Reformation, the contradiction between appearance and reality is
itself illusory. Their resolution is realized or made real in a miracle, that is, in an inexplicable reality. Yet in *Le Véritable Saint
Genest* this Catholic synthesis is in danger of breaking down into
its separate components: theater and church, play and ritual, sweet
and useful. Rotrou has made us lick the sugar-coated pill of
morality and has left us only to savor the memory or swallow the
pill.[5]

Chapter 4. Corneille. The Play as Magic

> FERDINAND: This is a most majestic vision, and
> Harmonious charmingly: May I be bold
> To think these spirits?
> PROSPERO: Spirits, which by mine art
> I have from their confines call'd to enact
> My present fancies.
>
> *The Tempest* (IV.i)

THE VIEW of the play as play did not go unchallenged by the partisans of the older view of the play as ritual. In the Middle Ages, ecclesiastical proscriptions had been invoked more against the actor than against the play he acted. For the very reason that the play was a ritual, the actor—sinner as he may have been—was not forbidden to worship through the art of playing. However, as the theater began to get a secular foothold in the France of the seventeenth century, ecclesiastical disapproval began to encompass not only the actor but the theater in all its aspects. Play as well as player began to be viewed as sinful. The play was a frank appeal to worldly interests and the theater in which it was played was at best a scene of diversion from more serious matters and at worst an occasion for the formation of dangerous liaisons. The didactic principle did not give way before the pleasure principle without a struggle.[1]

Nor without a compromise. Both sides, play lover and priest (often they were one), invoked the Horatian compromise of the "sweet and the useful." Many of the earliest *apologies du théâtre* are conceived with this compromise in mind. These defenses, however, are usually very defensive in tone—as for example, plays by Gougenot and Scudéry of the same name: *La Comédie des comédiens* (1633 and 1635 respectively). These playwrights, typically, apologize for the sweet; for them, as for Gillet de la Tessonerie in *Le Triomphe des cinq passions* (1642), the theater is primarily

47

a school for virtue. For the offensive in defense of the theater, of the sweet for its own sake, we turn to Corneille.

"Here," wrote Corneille in his dedication of *L'Illusion comique* (1636), "is a strange monster which I dedicate to you. The first act is but a prologue, the next three make up an imperfect comedy, the last is a tragedy: and all that, sewn together, makes for a play." [2] Most critics of the play have not looked beyond the first part of this indulgent characterization by its author: with varying degrees of indulgence on their own part, they have regarded *L'Illusion* primarily as "un étrange monstre." It has been dismissed as a youthful whim; taxed with superficiality and inconsistency; seen primarily as an *étude dramatique;* believed interesting only as a document of theatrical life in the period, a backstage curio; viewed as a dramatization of Corneille's relations with the actor Mondory, etc. Whatever the critical point of view (historical, biographical, moral, esthetic), the views of the play have all been partial. Many of these views are right, but right only when taken all together: this early play is an étude dramatique; a document of the stage controversy of the period; a whim, etc. It is, in short, a play about the theater.

> A présent le théâtre
> Est en un point si haut que chacun l'idolâtre,
> Et ce que votre temps voyoit avec mépris
> Est aujourd'hui l'amour de tous les bons esprits,
> L'entretien de Paris, le souhait des provinces,
> Le divertissement le plus doux de nos princes,
> Les délices du peuple, et le plaisir des grands;
> Il tient le premier rang parmi leurs passe-temps;
> Et ceux dont nous voyons la sagesse profonde
> Par ses illustres soins conserver tout le monde,
> Trouvent dans les douceurs d'un spectacle si beau,
> De quoi se délasser d'un si pesant fardeau.
> Même notre grand Roi, ce foudre de la guerre,
> Dont le nom se fait craindre aux deux bouts de la terre,
> Le front ceint de lauriers, daigne bien quelquefois
> Prêter l'oeil et l'oreille au Théâtre françois:
> C'est là que le Parnesse étale ses merveilles;

Les plus rares esprits lui consacrent leurs veilles;
Et tous ceux qu'Apollon voit d'un meilleur regard
De leurs doctes travaux lui donnent quelque part.
   D'ailleurs, si par les biens on prise les personnes,
Le théâtre est un fief dont les rentes sont bonnes;
Et votre fils recontre en un métier si doux
Plus d'accommodement qu'il n'eût trouvé chez vous.
Défaites-vous enfin de cette erreur commune,
Et ne vous plaignez plus de sa bonne fortune.   (v.v)

(At present, the theater is in such high esteem that everyone
adores it, and what your time saw with scorn is today the love
of all fine spirits, the talk of all Paris, the desire of the prov-
inces, the sweetest diversion for our princes, the delight of
the people, the pleasure of the mighty; it holds the first place
among their pastimes; and those whose profound wisdom we
know to guide the wide world find in the pleasures of such a
fine spectacle something to relax their burdened spirits. Even
our Great King, this mighty warrior, whose name is feared at
the ends of the earth, his brow wreathed in laurel, deigns
sometimes to lend an ear to the French Theater: It is there
that Parnassus displays marvels; the rarest spirits consecrate
their evenings to it, and all those whom Apollo looks upon
with favor give some portion of their learned efforts to it.
   Moreover, if one is to evaluate people by their possessions,
the theater is a fief from which the returns are good; and your
son finds in this so pleasant profession more well-being than
he would in yours. Rid yourself, then, of this common error
and complain no more of his good fortune.)

L'Illusion comique is written with this eulogy of the theater in
mind. The clear preoccupation with the theater in Act V only
makes explicit what is implicit in the preceding acts. Early in his
interview with the distraught father, Alcandre the magician promised Pridamant that he would see his son "plein de vie et d'honneur." Throughout the play, however, Pridamant is constantly
disturbed at the sight of his son in danger of death or in prison
or unfaithful. Alcandre's promise is apparently contradicted in
clearest fashion in Act v where Pridamant sees his "son" compromise both his wife and his benefactor, by making love to the

latter's wife—a treachery for which "Clindor" is killed. But the
treachery and the killing are not real, for Clindor is performing
such vile deeds only as he pursues the very lively ("plein de vie")
and most honorable ("et d'honneur") profession of actor. Furthermore, from the perspective of the revelation in Act v, the garments
which Alcandre evokes early in the play as belonging to the son
and the "coup de baguette" with which he evokes them are clearly
theatrical: they are, respectively, actor's costumes and the traditional system of warning that a play is about to begin. And a play
does begin: the play of Clindor's adventures in which the hero
acts himself. The spectator of the play is Pridamant; it is staged
in the depths of the grotto of the magician, who is, of course, both
playwright and *metteur-en-scène*. The purpose of the play is to
interest and please and, remembering the reason for Pridamant's
trip to the grotto theater, to reassure the spectator. Even as the
title of Scarron's *Le Roman comique* has been understood to mean
roman des comédiens, so *L'Illusion comique* can be understood to
mean *illusion des comédiens.*

From the very first line of the play we have been prepared for
this view of the characters of the play, particularly of Alcandre.
The magician is an artist: verse 1 (of the original edition) and
verses 7, 48, 88, 93, 127, and others make this equation of magician-
artist. Like the playwright-author, he selects events and arranges
them in a pattern calculated to interest and please his spectator.
The events which this magician-playwright selects are not real
events, but, *because of their very pastness,* illusory. And Alcandre
is an extremely Cornelian playwright: he cares little about the
unities of time and place. He reverses the natural course of events
so that we witness the present and the past in a single moment.
By sleight of hand the magician shifts his scene from grotto to
public square to prison to stage. As the magician is beyond physical laws of cause and effect, so the playwright is beyond their
esthetic counterpart of *vraisemblance.* Because his play is not a
regular comedy but a conjuration, his actors are but phantoms
and specters and they perform in a setting of mystery and awe, in
the "grotte obscure" which is his theater. His *double-entendres*
are so many black handkerchiefs to conceal his technique and ex-
cite the curiosity of the audience. His *coups de théâtre* are so many
tricks to delight and surprise the spectator. But being a magician

and not a necromancer, he is the first to admit (at the proper moment!) that his tricks are only tricks. As a good magician, Alcandre does not take his play seriously. To the extent, then, that Alcandre's conjuration is a play, the structure of *L'Illusion* is tripartite in its involutions: a play within a play within a play, the conjuration play being the middle term of the series.

The theme of the theater illuminates details of both language and structure. Clindor, Pridamant is told, "likes to make up before the public" (i.ii.144). Clindor has been the typical actor and jack-of-all-trades of the period: itinerant medicine man, public scribe, notary clerk, organ grinder, rhymester, seller of relics, quack doctor, solicitor. He has been, too, a "novelist," who wrote "songs for Gautier, conceits for Guillaume" (i.iii.181), these being common actors' names of the period. (The frequency of such allusions to the theater is too great for the theatrical connection to be merely coincidental.) Again, the theater is persistently evoked by one image in particular:

> Je vous le veux montrer plein d'éclat et de gloire
> Et la même action qu'il pratique aujourd'hui. (i.iii.202–3)

> (I want to show you him in all his brilliance and glory, in the very acts he is performing today.)

"Eclat" is constantly used to characterize the theater—or it does so retroactively after the revelation of Act v. In the enigmatic present of which Alcandre speaks to Pridamant, Clindor's fortune is "éclatante" (i.ii.126). In the last scene of Act iv, just before he evokes what will turn out to be a stage play, the magician tells Pridamant that he will have to create "fantômes nouveaux," for those under which he has shown Clindor up to that point "do not have enough brilliance for their conditions" (iv.x.1332). And upon seeing Isabelle as Hippolyte in the inner play (which he does not yet know is a play), Pridamant exclaims: "How Isabelle has changed, and how brilliant she is!" (v.i.1335) Finally, won over to respect for the theater by Alcandre, Pridamant says of it in Act v: "I did not know its brilliance, its utility, its charm" (v.v.1675). A potentially or semitheatrical language is also used to refer to Clindor's profession both before and after the revelation scene: "action" (i.iii.203) and "pratique" in the same line, as well as later in v.v.1618; "spectres parlants" (i.iii.212 and earlier: "spectres pareils," i.ii.152); "fantômes" (v.v.1628 and elsewhere), etc. Much of this language must be heard in context for its theatrical significance to be clear. The reader can gauge its prevalence from the citations given from the play.

Even more than details of language, details of structure demonstrate that *L'Illusion* is a play about the theater. The reactions of Pridamant to the "play" which Alcandre puts on for him in Acts ii–v are as integral to the over-all meaning of the play as his reactions to the stage play which he witnesses in Act v. Indeed, the reactions of Pridamant as spectator to both of the plays which Alcandre offers him constitute the primary play, the third term of the play within a play within a play. Pridamant's adventures provide the frame for those of his son not only in the peripheral acts of the entire play but in the peripheral scenes of each act. The prologue, as Corneille calls his first act, overflows its bounds to cover the whole play. Interesting in themselves, the events of Clindor's life after his banishment by Pridamant are also interesting for the effect on the repentant father and the sly magician. Through the exchange between these two, Corneille has included within the structure of his play esthetic considerations which usually remain external to the work of art; he has made explicit his dramatic principles; he has dramatized his dramaturgy. Through Alcandre the playwright gauges his effects on the spectator, Pridamant. He checks to see if he has achieved those effects which Georges May has described as Corneille's favorites: surprise and curiosity.[3] As Act ii ends with the plot against Clindor, we suddenly switch back to the primary plane of action where Alcandre observes to Pridamant: "Your heart is beating a little hard"; Act iii (or ii of Alcandre's play) ends with Clindor arrested for murder and we observe with Alcandre that this event has had the desired effect on the spectator: "How upset you are!"; Act iv (or iii of Alcandre's play) ends with Clindor's escape, to which the spectator makes the appropriate response: "At last, I can breathe"; Act v (or iv of Alcandre's play) begins with the surprising vision of Isabelle in a dazzling costume and the surprise has its effect: "How changed Isabelle is and how brilliant!"; Act v (or iv of Alcandre's play) ends with the magician-playwright offering his final surprise: Clindor, risen from the dead, counting his share in the play's profits. And, of course, the playwright has correctly gauged the result of this vision: "I see Clindor! Oh, Lord, what a strange surprise!"

These peripheral scenes, however, do more than bare the technique of Corneille; they also play a role in achieving his desired effects. They halt the action of Alcandre's play and thereby increase the anticipation and curiosity with which we await the revelations of the next act. Because of the excitement we feel at the end of each act, because of the anticipated revelations, we (that is, the spectators of whom Pridamant is the surrogate) miss the revelation which these peripheral scenes themselves contain: that what we have just witnessed and what we are about to witness are not real. We are meant to miss this revelation. Otherwise we would not be interested in the play, we would have no more to be curious and anxious about. Through these peripheral scenes, then, Corneille is also baring a more universal dramatic mechanism, the one by which the dramatist draws in or interests (Latin *inter + esse,* "to be in") the spectator: the mechanism of identification. The spectator feels *with* the character; he feels *for* the character. The blood relationship between Pridamant and Clindor, father and son, is a most telling symbol of the relationship between spectator and personage. Pridamant cannot hear Alcandre's reassurances because he is too affected by what is happening to his son. That he should be so affected keeps the play about Clindor's adventures, constructed as a flash back, moving forward in time. Through Pridamant Clindor's illusory adventures become real; through Alcandre they remain illusory.[4]

For this reason it is essential that there be no stage effect to disillusion Pridamant. Jouvet's 1937 staging of the last act, in which the play scene was played quite obviously as a play scene, with a theater interior erected on the stage and the play fragment presented in a spirit of parody, falsifies the play. Jouvet sensed the essential preoccupation with the theater in the play, but he misunderstood its meaning. Corneille's intention is certainly *in part* parodistic. Alcandre's early reproaches to fellow magicians (I.ii.127–32: "Les novices de l'art . . ."), for example, are really literary criticism. But the primary purpose of the play scene of the last act is to provide one more shock—and one more reassuring surprise—to Pridamant. Now, not even the dullest conception of the character of Pridamant could allow for his missing the point of the stage interior. Jouvet thus leaves for himself the difficult explanation of Pridamant's appeal to Alcandre at the moment of Théagène's death.

For Pridamant's appeal to Alcandre and the magician's reaction to it are the crux of the relationship between appearance and reality, between the events of the *comédie imparfaite* and those of the primary play on the one hand, and between these two and the tertiary play on the other. To Pridamant's appeal for help, Alcandre says nothing. There is no need to say anything. Nothing is wrong: Clindor's wound is not fatal, for it is not his wound. It is the wound of Théagène, of a "spectre" being represented by a "fantôme," a wound doubly unreal. For

> Son adultère amour, son trépas imprévu
> N'est que la triste fin d'une pièce tragique. (v.v.1632–3)

> (His adulterous love, his unforeseen ending are but the sad closing of a tragic play.)

Before this revelation all three planes of action have apparently collapsed: through the mechanism of identification, the primary plane of action (the adventures of Pridamant with the magician) has collapsed into the tertiary plane (Théagène's adventures); and the tertiary plane being, in Pridamant's eyes, but the continuation of the secondary (Clindor's adventures), the three planes of action have found a common focus in the father's anxiety. Alcandre's arch moralizing at "Clindor's death" seems to confirm that such a coalescence has occurred:

> Ainsi de notre espoir la fortune se joue:
> Tout s'élève ou s'abaisse au branle de sa roue;
> Et son ordre inégal, qui régit l'univers,
> Au milieu du bonheur a ses plus grands revers.
>
> (v.iv.1589–92)

> (Thus does fortune play with our hopes: everything goes up or down with the turning of its wheel; and its uneven order, which rules the universe, in the midst of happiness knows its greatest reversals.)

However, with the evocation of Clindor's "funérailles," the paying of the performers, the separate planes of action are disengaged from one another. The "pièce tragique" and Alcandre's conjuration play are seen for the illusions they are; the mechanism of identification breaks down: Pridamant cares little for an imaginary Théagène or a past Clindor.

The breakdown of identification is not complete, however. Ambiguous ties still link the primary and secondary planes of action (the breakdown from the tertiary is more complete). Because the acting of the "pièce tragique" occurs in the present, the secondary plane of action, of which it is an event, is in large part distinguished from the primary play: Alcandre was right to reassure Pridamant at every vision of Clindor in danger, for *that* Clindor was only a past, an illusory Clindor. Again, even in the reality of their presentness, the final scenes of Alcandre's play remain disengaged from the reality of Pridamant's own presence as a witness by the very fact that Clindor is actually not before his father: Pridamant reacts to an illusory actor, one acting within one remove from the father's plane of action. The real Clindor is in far-off Paris. But because the father has strong feelings about his son's *present* profession, the primary and secondary planes remain engaged; the mechanism of identification is still working. This *engagement* is made even stronger when Pridamant, his hostile feelings overcome by Alcandre, declares:

> Je n'ose plus m'en plaindre, et vois trop de combien
> Le métier qu'il a pris est meilleur que le mien.
>
> (v.v.1670–1)

(I dare complain no longer, and see too well how much better his profession is than mine.)

Pridamant announces that he will go to Paris and one wonders if it is not to join his son's acting company.

Does illusion triumph over reality? In this ambivalent relationship between the two planes of action does Corneille anticipate Pirandello? At the moment of the play within a play within a play the planes of *L'Illusion* threaten to collapse in a complete, in a Pirandellian manner. Pirandello, we recall, definitely flattens the planes of action from one end of *Sei personaggi* to the other: the members of the illusory family interrupt the real situation of actors rehearsing a play (no doubts about the reality of the primary plane: a rehearsal, not a performance). Pirandello's subject is not, or is not merely (as is the common view), the status of his fictional characters. For it is not only with the specialized problem of the autonomy of the artist's created characters that Pirandello is concerned. He is concerned, too, with the universal condition of man. Indeed, the two problems are inseparable, for the "imaginary" family knows a reality far more intense than that which their would-be interpreters could give them: they know the reality of life. This is the meaning of their autonomy, of their unedited experiences. Pirandello presents his conception of life through these "theatrical" characters (the family, who are not professionally of the theater) because the sufferings of this imaginary family are paradoxically more enduring, hence more convincing, than the disputes of the assembled actors about them. The playwright's subject, as Francis Fergusson has said, is "human life itself as theatrical." [5] Now, if in Pirandello fictional characters with their paradoxically greater reality interrupt a realistic plane, in Corneille fictional characters with their seemingly greater reality interrupt an illusory plane. The supernatural plane in Corneille seems very real, it is true: through its seeming reality we can measure the success of Corneille's magic. Yet the adventures of Clindor are as supernatural as those of the Théagène whom Clindor plays on the stage. We must place the adventures of Clindor in their proper secondary relationship to those of Pridamant. The penalty for failing to do so is to miss one of Corneille's most delightful *nouveautés:* the adventures of Clindor do not constitute the natural plane of action, but, being moments of Alcandre's conjuration play, are a part of a supernatural plane. Ultimately their reality, too, is only seeming.

Corneille's subject is not the theatricality of life but the theatricality of the theater. The events of Alcandre's play are real to Pridamant only because the latter does not listen to the magician's reassurances. Good playwright that he is, Alcandre counts on this deafness. The playwright abuses his spectator only for the sake of amusing that spectator. The play over, the playwright disabuses his spectator by admitting that it was only an illusion. Even to the extent that in *L'Illusion* the conjuration play is not over and the planes of action not disengaged (the actors being paid

are, after all, themselves only "fantômes"), the engagement does
not suggest a Pirandellian view. For Pirandello life is theatrical
before the playwright turns to it. For Corneille life is not theatrical but can become so. In *L'Illusion* we see Clindor becoming an
actor and we hear Pridamant attest to the superiority of his son's
calling to his own. Herein lies the principal danger of the whole
Cornelian theater: that the theatricality of the theater may be imposed on life itself, that the secondary plane invades the primary
plane. In *L'Illusion* there is no stage direction to indicate that the
toile which Alcandre had drawn and closed at various moments of
his conjuration is ever relowered on the final evocation of the paying of the actors.

To the extent, however, that Pridamant can distinguish between
his real son living in Paris and the *fantôme* evoking Clindor on
Alcandre's stage, the distance between the reality and the illusion
is maintained. The stage is a fiction. This view of the theater is
explicit and unambiguous in the relationship between the secondary and tertiary planes, between the adventures of Clindor
and those of Théagène. This relationship prefigures that between
the entire play and what can be called its fourth plane: the reality
in which the play occurs, in which we experience it. The esthetic
which *L'Illusion* develops turns toward the play to remind us that
L'Illusion is itself a play. Alcandre and Pridamant are themselves
"des spectres parlants." As magic, Corneille's play is one of those
rites which imitate their own ends. The end of all of the plays
which make up Corneille's play about the theater is to please.
The "éloge du théâtre" with which the play concludes makes this
clear. In Corneille's play about the theater, the Horatian compromise of the sweet and the useful has definitely been broken in
favor of the sweet. The theater is here defended primarily for its
ability to please: it is a *divertissement,* a *passe-temps,* a *délassement.*
It is Pridamant, Corneille's spectator, not Alcandre, Corneille's
playwright, who defends the theater on moral grounds: "I did not
know its brilliance, its utility, its charm" (v.v.1675). Even in this
momentary allusion, the useful is surrounded by the sweet (brilliance and charm). In Alcandre's long eulogy the only moral reference leaves edification completely out of the question: the theater
is a *relief* and an *escape* from the cares of state for the leaders of

the state (v.v.1652–6). Corneille, being an artist more concerned with the *art de plaire* than with the *art d'instruire,* might have adopted as his own *devise* the final words of Alcandre

> Servir les gens d'honneur est mon plus grand désir:
> J'ai pris ma récompense en vous faisant plaisir.
> Adieu: je suis content, puisque je vous vois l'être. (v.v.1683–5)

> (To serve people of honor is my greatest desire. I have found my reward in making you happy. Farewell: I am happy because I see you are.)

In *L'Illusion* the literary self-consciousness which Nadal has seen as characteristic of all of the early plays of Corneille reaches its greatest intensity.[6] The magician is a convention of the dramatic literature of the period, Corneille himself having used a magician in the play he wrote just prior to *L'Illusion, Médée.* The names of the principal characters of *L'Illusion* are stock names in the plays of the time and were used by Corneille frequently before and after this play: Alcandre (*Clitandre*), Dorante (*Le Menteur* and *Suite*), Géronte (*Clitandre* and *Le Menteur*), Isabelle (*Le Menteur*), Lyse (*Suite*), Hippolyte (*La Galerie du palais*), etc. Nor was Corneille the first to use the new convention of the inner play, Baro, Gougenot, and Scudéry all preceding him in its use. Again, the "comédie imparfaite," as Corneille described the play about Clindor's adventures, when taken in isolation resembles many other tragicomedies, the dominant genre in the period.

If the play is about the theater in general, it is also about the Cornelian theater in particular. *L'Illusion* contains many elements we think of as conventions of Corneille's dramaturgy. The *jeu de renonciation* between Hippolyte and Théagène looks forward to the famous passionate *combats amoureux* of the later plays (of the very next, *Le Cid*); Lyse, for all her Hermione-like fire, is a typically Cornelian heroine, creating for herself a new role which will allow her to transcend without contradiction her prior view of herself; Matamore's accents, rendered serious in another context, would not sound foreign on the lips of a Rodrigue. The open-ended structure of each act and of the play as a whole is a characteristic one, designed to produce the especially Cornelian effects of surprise and curiosity. This open-ended structure carries us, like all of Corneille's open-ended plays, beyond the outer frame even as the play ends. As much as it looks backward over his theater, *L'Illusion* looks forward to the plays which follow. We may suppose that the entire repertory of Cornelian heroes from Rodrigue to Suréna is being played by Clindor, even as it is Alcandre who creates that repertory for him. Is not Clindor the ideal actor to play those roles in which the hero constantly creates for himself a new role because of a new view of himself gained under the force of changing circumstances? Indeed, it is this perpetual *dépassement de soi* which is the essential dynamism of Cornelian dramaturgy. The macrocosm of the Cornelian world is fully articulated in the microcosm of *L'Illusion comique,* Corneille's eighth play, his own "prise de conscience théâtrale," his most brilliant "discours sur le poème dramatique."

The theater for its own sake, the theater only for the sake of pleasing: this is Corneille's statement of intention as an artist. But to please whom? There have been several answers to this question. For an older school of thought (led chiefly by Lanson) the playwright appealed largely to the stoical sensibility revitalized in the Renaissance. For others he appealed to the aristocratic and feudal sensibility inherited from the Middle Ages.[7] For E. B. O. Borgerhoff, a sensitive critic with a predilection for Racine and Pascal, Corneille is indifferent to such ethical preoccupations, for he is little more than a prestidigitator seeking only to astound his audience with his tricks.[8] Some scholars have described Corneille as a moment of the baroque,[9] a description which still another scholar has encompassed in a more far-reaching one: Corneille as a moment of the Counter Reformation.[10] Corneille does seem to speak for that confident Catholicism which, threatened by the Reformation, believes it can reconcile the two elements of the Western tradition judged incompatible by the Reformation: the classical view and the Christian view, this life and the eternal life, the sensible world and the suprasensible world, the esthetic and the ethical. Yet Corneille, if he does speak for such a view, does so primarily by underscoring the first term of these polarities: the classical view, this life, the sensible world, the esthetic. Corneille the dramatist seeks only to please.

Because he was educated by the Jesuits, the principal proponents of the Counter Reformational synthesis, the temptation is even greater to see a Jesuitical apologist in the dramatist. This proposes an inadequate view of the relationship between Corneille and his teachers. In the case of this highly self-conscious dramatist, as Nadal has demonstrated, the influences are largely literary. Corneille is as Jesuitical as the Jesuits are Cornelian. At most, we can say no more than that the Jesuitical morality of *la casuistique* corresponds to the anfractuous structure of Cornelian dramaturgy. The optimism and confidence of the Cornelian hero corresponds to the Jesuitical reliance on Molinistic views of man. The love of magic, of theatricalism, of "nouveauté" and "invention," in Corneille's words, is easily reconciled to a morality assimilating the two terms of the Western tradition. Indeed, Corneille's theater is not an effect but a part of that morality. And it is absolutely consistent that Corneille keeps the ethical and the esthetic separate. To paraphrase Pascal somewhat blasphemously, the order of art and the order of ethics are distinct but not contradictory. Corneille and the sensibility to which he appeals in his plays can "render unto Caesar the things which are Caesar's without denying unto God the things which are His." Thus there is no contradiction in a Corneille author of *L'Illusion comique* and a Corneille translator of the *Stabat Mater*. For Borgerhoff there are the beginnings of such a contradiction in the kind of translation Corneille makes, but Borgerhoff has let his opinion of Corneille's view of life—a fractured view according to the critic—obscure the *fact* of Corneille's translations of religious works. Confident of his God, sure of reality (Alcandre the playwright always knows the real from the unreal and so ultimately does the spectator), grateful to God for his genius, convinced that the world has been created by God to be enjoyed in all its beauty, Corneille writes those eulogies to human possibility we miscall his tragedies.

The theater of Corneille is not tragic in its view of life. Few critics have said this without attempting a Cornelian *jeu d'esprit* which will ultimately describe the dramatist as tragic. But tragedy, or a famous version of it, demands the destruction of value by value. In Corneille's dramas, however, the hero is not destroyed by a higher value nor even by an equal one, since value conflicts for the Cornelian hero are resolved in his, not his opponent's, favor. When they are not clearly resolved, as in the famous instance of *Le Cid,* not only is the hero not defeated, but there is the promise of his ultimate triumph. Least of all does the Cornelian hero represent the Aristotelian concept of defeat through the "tragic flaw." The heroes of Corneille have no tragic flaws; they know no limitations. There is no notion of the absurd to call forth a "counter-absurd," the assertion of man's greatness in spite of catastrophe. As one critic who has rejected the notion of a Corneille *tragique* has put it: "Tragedy? One should say, rather, tragicomedy or heroic comedy, as Corneille himself does sometimes; neither the heroes nor the climate of these plays are truly tragic; the tragic imposes upon man a limit and crushes him beneath an ineluctable force; the Cornelian hero knows no limit, he can do anything, not only overcome himself and others, but events, destiny itself; even death is at his command, like an instrument of his freedom." [11] Man can do anything: this is the key of the Cornelian outlook.

It is quite in keeping with this optimistic, confident, and humanistic outlook that Corneille should conceive his *apologie du théâtre* in *L'Illusion comique* less as a self-conscious defensive than as a self-congratulatory offensive. The offensive is grounded in a sure conviction of what is real as well as in a sure conviction of the benevolence of the unreal. The benevolent magic of Alcandre replies to the destructive magic of Médée in the tragedy by that name of the preceding year. It is as if Corneille wished to reassure us in *L'Illusion* that even Médée's magic, however malevolent it may have seemed, was really stage magic too, harmless and only "pour vous faire plaisir." In Eric Bentley's careful distinction between the serious and the playful use of magic, Corneille's is a magic of *as if*—"as if real contact were made with another realm." [12] Sure of his values, the artist does not confuse appearance and reality except to the extent that he deliberately does so in order to please. "Ne . . . que" is the saving principle of Corneille's view of the relation between art and life: the illusion is *only* illusion. More significantly, the illusion is *comique*. "All that, sewn together," we might say of the theater of Corneille, "makes for a comedy."

Chapter 5. Molière. The Play as Mask

> And let those that play your clowns
> speak no more than is set down for
> them; for there be of them that will
> themselves laugh, to set on some barren
> spectators to laugh too, though in the
> mean time some necessary question of
> the play be then to be considered; that's
> villainous and shows a most pitiful am-
> bition in the fool that uses it.
>
> *Hamlet* (III.ii)

IT IS but a short step from Corneille to Molière—from the notion of art as a separate, if secondary, sphere of interest to the notion of art as an autonomous sphere on an equal footing with the
ethical. And, in Molière himself, it is a still shorter step from
the autonomy of the esthetic as it is expressed in *L'Impromptu de
Versailles* (1663) to the assimilation of the ethical into the esthetic
in *Le Malade imaginaire* (1673).

I

L'Impromptu de Versailles is Molière's final thrust in the long
literary quarrel which began with his *L'Ecole des femmes,* first
shown December 26, 1662. He had already replied to much of
the calumny provoked by that play in his *Critique de L'Ecole des
femmes* (first shown June 1, 1663). Yet the attacks, led by two
minor writers, Donneau de Visé and Boursault, continued, shifting from the more or less professional level to the personal. When
they began to touch upon Molière's relations with his young wife
half his age, the dramatist decided it was time to reply more directly. He did so in the form of a *comédie des comédiens,* thereby
finding the occasion not only to reply to the particular attacks
which had been made upon him but to place in proper ethical
and esthetic perspective the relationship of the artist's private to

his professional life. The "backstage play" or comédie des comédiens is a favorite of the seventeenth-century French theater.
Indeed, Corneille's *L'Illusion comique* and Rotrou's *Saint Genest*
are comédies des comédiens, although it would be an inadequate
criticism which would consider them as merely interesting documents of the theater conditions of their times. Exclusive interest
in the documentary aspect of such plays undoubtedly reflects one
of the principal appeals of a comédie des comédiens; its apparent
realism. The actor seems to drop the mask, to present himself as a
person instead of a personage. Yet the seeming is the heart of the
matter here as in any other play. The formula involves a double-
take: the actor wears the mask of an actor.

As Molière does, for example, in *L'Impromptu de Versailles*.
This play has so often been regarded in relation to the polemics
of which it is but one moment that it has hardly been examined
in its own rights as a brilliant play. The virulence and fervor of
the battle deriving from Molière's supposed indelicacies in *L'Ecole
des femmes* have led too many critics to treat *L'Impromptu* not
as an illusion of reality but as reality itself. It is a Molière who
has dropped the mask, we are told by one critic, the offended
husband who speaks with a measured gravity in reply to his
prurient enemies.[1] It is, another critic tells us, a hurt Molière who
takes the boards in order to reply to his enemies in his own
name, one who abandons the weapons of the writer and the
subtleties of the court playwright, one who thinks aloud his utmost
pain and anger.[2] These and like-minded critics see and hear in
L'Impromptu not the author charged with indelicacy before the
public but the cuckolded husband.

More perceptive critics have taken a less simplistic view of the
play. Michaut, for example, has sensed that the relations between
the various actors (he has in mind particularly Molière's rejoinder
to Mlle Molière: "You are stupid, my dear wife") are dictated
not by biographical but by dramatic impulses. Molière appears
brusque, impatient, and angry because the *donnée* of the play
requires it: a calm or apathetic Molière would have destroyed the
supposition which the play poses that not only Molière but the
whole troupe is upset and harried both by the increasing bitter-
ness of the attacks upon it and by the need to provide on-the-spot
entertainment for the king.[3] And a Danish critic, Valdemar Vedel,

has been even more concerned with the internal aspects of the play: the play both presents and is itself a statement of a realistic esthetic. Molière strips away all the illusion by presenting a group of actors rehearsing. "With still more audacity," writes Vedel, "reality and contemporary life were put on the stage, transformed more than ever into a public tribunal." [4] And of Molière's theater in general, Vedel has maintained that the principal theme is "the play between stupidity and ruse." [5] A recent English critic, W. G. Moore, has heeded Lanson's long-established insistence on Molière's viewpoint as an actor and has concluded that *L'Impromptu* is one of the dramatist's many "experiments with dramatic illusion . . . a sign of this actor's constant preoccupation with the actor's chief problem, that of communication across the footlights." [6] Finally, Vedel has provided a more general clue to a new interpretation of *L'Impromptu:* "Comedy is the kind of ruse which Molière employs by preference. To put on a play within a play, to play a character who in turn is playing another, there, certainly, is something to satisfy in Molière the demon of the theater." [7] Bringing the views of these critics to bear on Molière's comédie des comédiens, we can perhaps see that far from letting the mask drop, he has more firmly than ever attached it to his face.

It is Molière's genius, Ramon Fernandez tells us, to describe the gap between "le vouloir" and "l'imaginé." [8] It is described, however, not—as the critic suggests in a general rule for Molière comedy—through the dropping of a mask but through the assumption of one. For example, Toinette (of *Le Malade imaginaire*) unmasks Béline by having Argan assume the mask of death: that is, the wish to expose the false Béline can be satisfied only by an act of imagination. Furthermore, in the case of Molière himself as he appears in *L'Impromptu,* the gap between wish and imagination, between unfulfilled desire and fulfilled desire, is even closed by this process. For traditionally, as in the Italian theater before Molière, each actor had his mask, a fixed role which he invariably played under the mask designating a type. This meant, as Lanson demonstrated sometime ago, that each actor had three names: "Un nom réel, un nom de théâtre, et un nom de farce." [9] Some typical cases: Robert Guérin, called La Fleur, called Gros Guillaume; Henri le Grand, called Belleville, called Tur-

lupin. In time this last name, the "nom de farce," became itself
a mask, the name by which the actor came to be known. The implications for the Molière, who appears in *L'Impromptu* are clear:
Jean Baptiste Poquelin, called Molière, called Molière. The gap
between wish and imagination is closed as the wish is fulfilled in
the work of the imagination: we see not Poquelin, the offended
man, but Molière, the mask Poquelin wears (or wishes to wear)
even in society, the mask of the artist over the face of the man.

Abused as an artist, it is as an artist that Molière replies. In
so doing he has given a valuable insight into his creative activity.
In their commendable effort to describe the sources of Molière's
genius in his acting, most critics have gone too far afield with their
excursions into the *commedia dell'arte* or the farce tradition or
eyewitness accounts, etc.[10] There is in *L'Impromptu* perhaps all
the evidence we need that in Molière the author is inseparable
from the actor and practical man of the theater. Molière creates
and feels his characters as he acts out their roles in the process of
creation. Pressed by De Brie to give the troupe an idea of the
comédie des comédiens he has so often been forced to postpone,
the author-director gives an *ébauche* in which he plays all the roles.
(It is typical of Molière's irony that he should regret not giving
his play about the theater in his play about the theater.) He is thus
enabled to parody the acting styles of his rivals: Beauchâteau,
Hauteroche, Villiers, and others. Now, much has been made of
Molière's insistence on the natural in acting, an insistence heard
earlier in the century in Hamlet's advice to the actors. Certainly
the outlandishness of the so-called Cornelian style stands out in
stark contrast to the simplicity of Molière's own style as he discusses acting problems with the troupe. One has only to have eyes
to see with in order to appreciate the superiority of the natural.
Nevertheless, for all this insistence on the natural, Molière's
naturalism is not the literal-mindedness which goes by that name
in the late nineteenth century. If the playwright turns to the everyday reality of salon society or to the exact conditions of his professional life, the conventions within which his plays are realized are
not predominantly social or realistic; they are dramatic. Naturalism
for Molière is not an end; it is a technique, a means of reinforcing
the illusion of reality, not of replacing reality. The reality which
is uppermost in his mind is that of the stage.

As a director, Molière seems to belong to the be-yourself school; he seems to favor what might be called an *esthétique de convenance:* the actor plays that role most like his own personality. In *L'Impromptu* the director assigns to each member of the troupe the role which, as far as we can tell from evidence outside of the play, does closely conform to the personality of the performer. Some critics tell us that the first person to perform according to these strictures is Molière himself. And certain Molière editors believe that he thus characterizes a number of his fellow actors as well: Brécourt, for example, whom Molière asks to strive for "un air posé" and to gesticulate as little as is possible for him, is known to have been of a violent, outlandish nature; Mlle Du Croisy, asked to play the role of a scandalmonger, is herself known to have had quite a mean tongue.[11] The case of Mlle Du Parc poses the esthetic problem of the actor's personality in a crucial way, so we might go into it at some length in order to learn something of Molière not only as a director but as a dramatist as well.

Du Parc had the reputation of a *façonnière* ("an affected person"). In the play, Molière apparently makes great fun of this failing in the actress:

> MADEMOISELLE DU PARC: Good Lord, for my part, I shall acquit myself very poorly of my role. I do not know why you gave me this role of an affected woman.
> MOLIÈRE: Good Lord, Mademoiselle, that's the way you talked when you got your role in the *Criticism of the "School for Wives";* yet you acquitted yourself marvelously then, and everyone agreed that no one could have been better than you. Believe me, this one will be the same way, and you will play it better than you think.
> MADEMOISELLE DU PARC: How can that be done? For there is none in the world less affected than I.
> MOLIÈRE: That is true; and that's why you will be better able to show what an excellent actress you are, by portraying so well a character who is your very opposite. Try then, all of you, to take on the character of your roles and to imagine yourselves ["de vous figurer"] what you are portraying.
> (scene i)

It is a passage such as this which has led the above-mentioned critics to establish an identification between the Du Parc of the play and the historical Du Parc of Molière's company. We should not be fooled by the surface of Molière's words, they tell us, for he is here being ironical: the real Du Parc is affected, but you cannot expect Molière to get her to be something she thinks she is not by telling her point-blank that she is that very thing. Molière actually tells us through his irony that in becoming something you think you are not, you become yourself: "In Molière," the realistic critic might put it, "to assume the mask is really to doff the mask."

Nevertheless, even this subtle probing of the mask in Molière remains superficial. A quarter of a century ago, Michaut cautioned against the identification between the stage actors and the real actors. Only the *données* of the dramatic situation, not those of real life, govern the relations between the members of the troupe in *L'Impromptu:* the director is short-tempered not so much because of the subject of his play (a reply to Boursault's vicious *Portrait du peintre*) as because he has been called upon to do it before the king almost without notice. The realism of the situation thus consists less in the accuracy of the portraits than in the director's attempt "to distribute the roles while making everybody happy, and to have actors adapt themselves exactly to the roles assigned them." [12] The notion of adaptation suggests an esthetic very different from an *esthétique de convenance,* one rather in which the actor plays a role *not* necessarily suited to his personality. In fact we hear Molière subscribe to such an esthetic more than once in the play. "This will constrain you a little," he tells Du Parc when she rebels against her assignment, "but what can be done about it? Sometimes one has to do oneself violence." Only more irony, the realist retorts. Indeed yes, but irony of a very special kind, one which "ironizes" what we think of as irony in the ordinary sense. One critic of modern poetry has defined this very special irony in these terms: "In matter-of-fact discourse, the understanding of the ironic remark as the opposite of the expected one is sufficient. But in the further reaches of connotative language it becomes clear that what is opposite on one level of significance may be apposite on another. In a poem a word or group of words may have more than one meaning." [13] In *L'Impromptu* the unexpected or opposite element in the ironic complex is Molière's acceptance of the actress' view of herself. Expecting overt contradiction, we get overt confirmation—the latter presumably

unjustified. At a deeper level, however, the confirmation is justi-
fied, for Molière primarily wishes to project on the stage not
Du Parc's person but the personage of the play. The director
wishes less to expose the actress than to compose a role; he is interested in her not as she is but as she might be. In the shaping
of his illusion the director must objectively contend with the
subjectivity of the actress, for her views of herself are quite as
real as other views of her. Even granting that Molière wishes to
expose the affectedness of Du Parc, are not the means—the effort
of the creative self he demands of her—as important as the
ends? The actress' feeling that she will have to *try* to be affected
is quite sincere and so is the director's advice to her: "Il faut
parfois se faire violence." The violence involves an effort of imagination and an act of will through which Du Parc will become another without ceasing to be herself; Molière's advice is not sarcasm
but wisdom.

In *L'Impromptu* the great comedian is just as objective about
his own roles. He does not present what we have come to regard
as a Pirandellian twist: a play about a man directing a play in
which he plays himself. Quite to the contrary, he keeps the self
of the play proper, Molière the director, distinct from the self
of the play within a play, the foppish marquis. True, Molière
does apparently destroy the illusion by several times placing his
own name on the lips of the ridiculous marquis he himself is
portraying:

> LA GRANGE: Let us call out our names to the doorkeeper, so
> that he can announce us.
> MOLIÈRE: That's fine for you, but for my part, I don't want
> to be made fun of ["être joué"] by Molière.   (scene iii)

But the fact that the fop is, nonetheless, "joué par Molière" both
figuratively by the author and literally by the actor only underscores the versatility of the mask in Molière: he can through his
art become like those least like him without ceasing to be himself.
To insist either that Molière has ceased to be himself in order to
become the marquis (the romantic delusion) or that he is only
Molière while playing the marquis (the positivist simplification) is
to sacrifice the doubleness which is the essence of Molière's vision.
For he becomes the marquis not through complete immersion

in the role but through what might be described as *dédoublement voulu,* the deliberate multiplication of the self. "Tâchez de vous figurer," ("Try to imagine yourselves") we have heard him advise his troupe—not "tâchez d'être" ("try to be"). The effort of imagination involves not an *abandon de soi au rôle,* but rather an application of the will, a constant consciousness of the directing sensibility.

In the inner play and the play proper Molière wears a mask. In each, the author-director maintains the debate at the objective level of art. When Béjart in the play proper and Climène in the play within a play try to wage the debate at the irrelevant level of private lives, Molière in the main play and "le marquis honnête homme" in the inner play propose an impersonal debate on the professional and esthetic questions provoked by *L'Ecole.* Moreover, though the debate is the same in each plane of action, it is never conducted in Pirandellian crisscross fashion: Béjart out of character does not argue with the imaginary marquis who defends Molière, and Climène of the play within a play does not debate with Molière the director. The planes of action remain distinct, and when they threaten to merge Molière the director stops the rehearsal. This autonomous relationship describes Molière's desire for objectivity more persuasively than any discursive statement of it.

If the members of the troupe had their way, of course, the planes of action would not remain distinct. They criticize Molière for being too tame, for sparing in their persons those who had attacked him as a person in a professional quarrel. Thus the shadows of those slanderers, if not their very presences, intrude momentarily into the impersonality of the stage. But to the troupe's demand that he reply in kind to his enemies, Molière sternly counters:

. . . Courtesy must have its limits; and there are some things which make neither the spectators nor him of whom one speaks laugh. I gladly give over to them [i.e., my enemies] my works, my face, my tone of voice, and my manner of speaking, for them to do with them what they will, if they can draw some advantage in doing so; I am not opposed to all these things and I would be enchanted if these could make people happy. But in giving them all that, they should grant me

the grace of leaving the rest and of not touching upon matters of the nature of those upon which, I am told, they have
been attacking me in their plays. This is what I would ask
quite civilly of that respectable gentleman who bothers about
writing for them, and there is all the reply they shall have of
me.   (scene v)

This is the closest we come to seeing and hearing something of
the man, of the offended husband. But as in the case of the
médisants who provoke him, we see not the husband but the
shadow he casts. The shadow is quickly banished as the artist calls
once again for the direct and impersonal lighting of the stage. On
the stage we perceive only the mask.

   Molière thus attaches a positive connotation to the idea of mask.
Does *L'Impromptu* offer, then, an exception to W. G. Moore's
analysis of the mask in Molière? "The deceiver, or the fool, or the
doctrinaire prides himself on his wits, his ideas, his reason. He
leaves his instinct out of the reckoning; he adopts a mask of intelligence. But instinct will be revenged and returns unexpectedly;
the mask has to fall." [14] Or does *L'Impromptu* provide the rule
rather than the exception? We might here point out that it is not
the rationalistic but often the instinctual types who wear the mask
in Molière (the young men and women, the peasants who so often
frustrate the monomaniacs through clever devices). For all its
subtlety Moore's analysis of the mask in Molière suffers from a
basic misunderstanding. To say that in each of his great monomaniac figures Molière shows us the "mask of [his] delusion" is
to be self-contradictory,[15] for a mask is a second face *consciously*
worn. The monomaniac does not regard his obsession as a delusion; by definition, he does not realize that more objective at-
titudes toward it are possible. He expresses the sincere rigidity of
self-obsession, not the ironic rigidity of the mask. And rarely in
Molière does the comic figure overcome his delusion, so that if, as
Moore's analysis implies, a Molière play moves inexorably toward the moment of unmasking, it is not toward the unmasking
of the victim but of the victors, who doff the mask because it has
now served its purpose. It might even be doubted that such is the
inexorable movement of Molière dramaturgy. In the case of
L'Impromptu, the vision which Molière insists be presented is

not that of Poquelin but that of Molière, the mask of the artist over the face of the man. Like his contemporary Vermeer, Molière in his canvas of *An Artist in His Studio* concerns himself with the act of creation, with the painting and not the painter. Molière's mask, like the painter's back, denies us a portrait of the man.

II

It is especially difficult for us to grasp the notion of the mask as an affirmation of value. Semantically, *mask* falls into a negative field, one mined with such pejorative notions as *hide, conceal, disguise, deceive, fool, falsify, cheat,* etc. Yet by his positive conception of the mask as the properly impersonal vehicle of dramatic art, Molière in *L'Impromptu* has succeeded in neutralizing many of these pejorative connotations. The mask of art, he tells us in this play, does not so much conceal the personal life as make it irrelevant.

Nevertheless, one feels that the dramatist has at best succeeded only in neutralizing the negative connotations, not in reversing them. If the play, in its intrinsic value as an *art poétique,* reveals much about Molière's art, it does so in a restrictive and defensive way. Like a lover's quarrel, the play has the interest but also the limitations of its specialized concerns; Molière seems to have much to say to his fellow artists, less to his fellow men. As he speaks to his fellow artists, we feel that the negative accent is as pronounced as the affirmative. Exposing the false conceptions of art held by his enemies, Molière states his own positive conceptions defensively at best. The objective, professional anger which Molière expresses near the end of the play is still anger, a negative, not a positive, emotion. *L'Impromptu* represents that order of comedy of which Baudelaire believed Molière to be the finest French expression: "le comique significatif" which the great poet-critic defines as "a language more clear, more easily understood by the common run of men, and especially easier to analyze, its elements being visibly double: art and moral idea . . ." [16] In his comédie des comédiens Molière reads a lesson in professional ethics to his fellow artists: things should be kept at the level at which they began, the level of art or mask.

In his late work, however, the dramatist succeeds in reversing the pejorative connotations of *mask,* making the symbol affirmative and triumphant. In *Le Bourgeois Gentilhomme* and in *Le Malade imaginaire* the masked ballets which terminate the plays formalize the triumph of the mask: as if in sign of their victories, the victors keep their masks on. In the final *intermèdes* of these plays, Baudelaire believed, Molière went beyond le comique significatif in order to achieve the highest form of the comic, *le comique absolu,* which the poet-critic defines as "a creation crossed by a certain faculty imitative of elements pre-existing in nature" and which he sees as the product of a "prodigious poetic good humor." [17] The concluding "Ballet des nations" of *Le Bourgeois* and the final mock investiture of *Le Malade* are permanent expressions of this "humor," miniature plays within plays put on not merely at the expense of but for the sake of Jourdain and Argan.

In *Le Malade* the mock investiture is more than just figuratively like a play, for it is formally played by the actors Béralde has invited, those who have already entertained Argan (Intermède, end of Act II). But also now formally assuming the mask of art in the mock investiture are those "actors" who had earlier informally assumed the mask of ruse: Cléante and Angélique, who had pretended to be playing an *opéra comique* in order to make love before Argan, because he disapproved their love; Toinette, who had arranged various little pretenses to prove to Argan the double-dealing of his doctors and his wife. The final comedy within a comedy thus provides a structural metaphor for the theme of double identity which Moore sees as central in *Le Malade* and which, following Vedel, we might see as central in all of Molière. The comedy of the mock investiture presents Molière's world in microcosm, a world in which, to quote Béralde, "all this is but between us. We, too, can take on roles in it and thus put on a play for ourselves." The whole thing is between us—among the human lot of us. As for the person who is the butt of the comedy: "It is not so much to make fun of him as to accommodate ourselves to his fantasies" (III.xiv).

Accommodation to fantasy: this is surely a comic view. Yet there have been those who would transform Molière into a tragic poet. The desire to do so derives from two related tendencies in Molière criticism: the first to view the plays as reflections of his society, the second to view them as autobiographical documents. These views have led to the familiar dichotomies of town or bourgeois plays versus court or aristocratic plays, satire versus fantasy, morality versus poetry, etc.—the former terms usually designating "major" works, the latter "minor." At the basis of these divisions, André Le Breton has seen the bourgeois, liberal ethos of the nineteenth century, for liberal critics insist on a Molière critic of the *ancien régime.* Yet, Le Breton notes, the *comédies-ballets,* traditionally said to constitute the bulk of the "minor" work, make up nearly one-half of the Molière canon.[18] More recently, Paul Bénichou (*Les Morales du grand siècle*) has seen in all of the canon a Molière nearer to the affirmative and outgoing Corneille than to the satirical, reductive La Rochefoucauld. As for the autobiographical view of the plays, the romantic Molière of bitter laughter, we have tried to show that it is against this very kind of identification that *L'Impromptu* does battle. La Grange's well-known denial notwithstanding, he may have been "a melancholy dreamer," but these personal qualities have not spilled over into the plays. Because they cannot see the play for their documents, autobiographical critics have had a heyday studying the relationships between *Le Malade* and Molière's fatal stroke while playing in it. But the tragic poet, if there is one in Molière, grieves off in the wings, while the comic poet dances for us onstage.

For, in spite of André Gide, this play is not a "farce tragique." [19] It is a comedy. Molière, it must be repeated, is a comic poet. His insight into the relationship between appearance and reality differs radically from that of a Sophocles. The comic "hero" makes no discovery of reality; there are, as it has variously been said, no conversions in Molière. It is not the comic hero's view of reality which prevails, for a Molière comedy offers us the triumph of those we can best describe as "the others." Which others? For a long while, in the day of the liberal critics cited by Le Breton, it was believed to be of the Philintes or *raisonneurs,* the advocates of the golden mean. Recent reactions to such a view claim that the triumph has been of the natural, represented by peasant types and the young. Bénichou has even conceived of Molière comedy as a kind of pincer movement in which the extremes of natural peasant and freedom-loving aristocrat crush the intimidated, socially

anxious bourgeois. Yet such political approaches, however valid
historically, remain at best peripheral to any attempt to understand Molière as an artist.

The question remains: Who are "the others" who triumph in
Molière comedy? The burden of our analysis leads us to reply, those
who are willing to assume a mask. A Molière comedy is an appeal to
awareness, an appeal always provoked by the lack of awareness in the
comic figure. "The others" thus define the degree and nature of the
comic figure's limitations. The true hero of a comedy is, in fact, "the
others," and their view ought more appropriately to be compared
with that of the tragic hero in any discussion of the tragic and the
comic. Critics too often draw a contrast between the doubleness of
vision of the tragic hero and the singleness of vision of the comic
hero so-called. But a comedy is not without its doubleness of vision,
as we can see in the reactions called for in "the others" by the monomania of the central figure. The comic "others" are ready to assume a mask, they are willing to play a double game. The central
figure (an Argan, an Harpagon) simply cannot play such a game,
for he does not know of its possibility. Ironically, the tragic hero
yearns for the singleness of vision of the comic figure, for whom
appearance and reality coincide. However, if the tragic figure and
the comic "others" are alike in their doubleness of vision, they
differ in the very essence of that vision: where the tragic hero
sees discrepancy and even duplicity, the comic "others" see combination and complementarity—of the social and the natural, of
the logical and the illogical, of the conditioned and the instinc-
tive, of the material and the spiritual.

"Why," asks Pascal, "is custom not natural? I am very much
afraid that [this] nature is itself only a first custom, even as custom
is a second nature." [20] And Molière, without being very much
afraid of the identification, replies with Scapin and Toinette and
Béralde. For the "customary" Béralde is as "natural" as the "natural" Toinette is "customary." Toinette is not a simple child of
nature, but in her penchant for ruse is closer to Tartuffe than to
some Rousseauistic natural man. And it is the artful Béralde who
ceaselessly urges faith in nature on the would-be invalid. Both
Toinette, the so-called voice of nature, and Béralde, the so-called
voice of society and reason, put on a comedy for Argan. In so doing, like the Molière of L'Impromptu, they propose to us the specif-

ically comic response to the problem of human limitation: in the face of such limitation we are invited to seek solutions through the assumption of a series of masks. When the limitation seems irreducible, as in the case of Argan's monomania, we are asked to assume the mask nevertheless and thus to accommodate ourselves to human limitations. Argan's mania acts then not as a narcotic but as a stimulant: it becomes the occasion of a play. Béralde tells his fellow men what the Molière of *L'Impromptu* tells his fellow actors: Become another self even while remaining your old self. "In Molière," we might reply to those who see in him only the satirist, "to assume the mask is to free oneself." The comic vision insists on the multiplicity of life and is no more escapist for doing so than the tragic vision with its emphasis on human finitude is defeatist.

In the comédie-ballet, the astute Fernandez tells us, Molière achieves the fullness of his comic vision: "Ballet is for comedy what death is for tragedy: the leap into the beyond, the fulfillment of the trajectory, a flight carried through, without a return, without an artificial reaccommodation to the optics of the 'real world.' " [21] A ballet is the perfect expression of the human: movement plus form, movement become gesture. As part of the architectonic structure of a Molière play, the ballet is "a dance within a mirror." Like the poet in Cocteau's *Orphée*, Molière invites us to plunge into this mirror. Unlike Prospero's, Béralde's powers only begin to manifest themselves as the play ends. "Our revels," he might paraphrase from Prospero, "now are *begun*" and, addressing himself to the audience, "now my charms are all o'er grown / And what strength I have's *your* own." For Molière invites us to the esthetic point of view, "the only one," says Gide, "which is not exclusive of all the others." [22] The natural Toinette of *Le Malade* and the naive Agnès of *L'Ecole des femmes* overcome the stubborn pretensions of Argan and Arnolphe through the artifices of ruse and mask. The natural speaks through the conventional, as is only appropriate in that world which is a triumph of art, a triumph of the human—the world of Molière.

Chapter 6. Marivaux. The Play as Game

> The effect of my intent is to cross theirs
> They do it but in mocking merriment
> And mock for mock is only my intent.
> *Love's Labour Lost* (v.ii)

THE SUPERIMPOSITION of the real intrigue over the illusory one, which was a miracle in Rotrou and an enchantment in Corneille, becomes in much eighteenth-century comedy a stratagem. People play with a purpose; the game is played for keeps. The formal breaks down into the informal, parallel lines of development are suddenly made to converge. An autonomous play is used, because of its adaptability, to more realistic ends—usually a marriage over the heads of unwilling parents, such as we have seen, for example, in Shakespeare's *Merry Wives*. Yet for the most part, the victim of the ruse is content to be fooled in such a way. The *démon du théâtre* having possessed nearly everyone in this, the most social, the most conventional of centuries, there is no pique in his tone as the *joué* suddenly realizes that "on m'a donné la comédie" ("you've put on a play at my expense"). Rather, he enjoys the play and consents to the marriage simply because it has been a play, one in which he makes the denouement truly comic by his accommodation to the fantasy. It is no longer a question of the sweet *or* the useful: the sweet *and* the useful are viewed as complementary. This is, of course, a secularized version of the sugar-coated pill of morality which had been the traditional ecclesiastical approach to art. But there has been a shift in emphasis from the pill to the coating. Reality is more theatrical than the stage. Life itself is a comedy and is to be enjoyed as such. The stratagem is conceived in the spirit of the game; the purpose of playing is almost exclusively playing. This outlook, a heritage of the Molière of *Le Malade imaginaire,* is best represented in the finest playwright of the age: Marivaux.

Recent editors of Marivaux, nurtured on Pirandello and imbued with Jean Anouilh, have admired the subtlety and daring
of the playwright's speculation in one act, *Les Acteurs de bonne
foi,* believed to have been written, though not produced, in 1757.[1]
In it, they believe, Marivaux is studying the conflict of the actor:
the struggle between life and art, the "interpenetration between
feigned reality and true reality." The inevitable evocation of
Pirandello is forthcoming, though it is misleading here in its implication of similarity. Marivaux is no more of a "half-way Pirandello" than he is, in the frequent interpretation, a "half-way
Racine." The significance of Marivaux's interest in the conflict
between art and life is that it is not pushed any further than it is
in *Les Acteurs.* Marivaux, it is true, is concerned in this play
with the same order of speculation as Pirandello in *Questa sera si
recita a soggetto,* but his speculations differ profoundly from those
of Pirandello.

In this order of speculation the question of the *comédie de
société* which is the subject of *Les Acteurs* goes beyond simple considerations of satire. Marivaux probably finds Mme Amelin's addiction to the theater ridiculous—as ridiculous, in fact, as Mme
Argante's opposition to it. But it is not with the correction or
even the simple presentation of this vice that Marivaux is concerned in this play. It is with virtue that he is concerned, with
the two reciprocal virtues which are indeed the dominant concerns of his whole theater: *comédie* and *société.* For society is a
comedy or a succession of comedies in the world of Marivaux.
Les Acteurs is typical in this respect, for in it the figurative notion of "se donner la comédie," ("putting on a play for each
other"), the notion at the basis of *Le Jeu de l'amour et du hasard,*
of *La Surprise de l'amour,* of *Les Sincères,* becomes literal. The
relationships of Merlin's little impromptu are those of *La Double
Inconstance:* the love between Merlin and Lisette, like that between Arlequin and Sylvia, is really an affair of convention and
habit; the one between Merlin and Colette in the inner play, like
that between the prince and Sylvia, is born of free and sincere
feeling. The pattern, though essentially the same, is varied, of
course, for in the Merlin impromptu, Blaise, unlike Arlequin, is
not compensated with a Flaminia. But this is still a variation (by
omission), not a reversal of formula. Again, the breakdown of the

formal into the informal is the movement (or one of the movements) of Merlin's impromptu, as it is too of *La Surprise de
l'amour* in which the love between the countess and Lélio is
born of "a comedy they give one another." The sense of confusion
and despair felt by Lisette and Blaise at the end of the rehearsal
scene parallels that moment of a Marivaux comedy in which the
hero or heroine, confused by the real commitment he or she has
made while "playing the comedy," laments: "Who is safe from what
is happening to me? Where are we in all this?" (Sylvia, in *Le Jeu de
l'amour et du hasard,* II.vii) Finally, the dropping of the masks
and the movement toward equilibrium which are characteristic
aspects of Marivaux dramaturgy, are also characteristic of *Les
Acteurs.*

On the surface, the fictional and the real in Marivaux are in a
symbiotic relationship. The barrier between the supposed and the
actual is unstable and constantly breaking down. Thus the simulated love of Merlin and Colette produces real anger and jealousy
in Blaise and Colette, even though they know that they are only
witnessing a play. The structure of Merlin's impromptu is such
that even the offstage spectator is made to forget Merlin's admission to Eraste that he and Colette are "both agreed to see what
Blaise and Lisette will do upon hearing all the sweet things we
pretend to be saying to one another; the whole thing put on to
see if they won't be upset and jealous." During the rehearsal
Lisette and Blaise (and at times Colette) frequently interrupt
the performance; the real exchanges between the actors are as
frequent, in fact, as the fictional, and often as lengthy. The crisscross pattern of the exchanges—from Merlin onstage to Blaise
offstage, from Colette offstage to Blaise onstage, from the real
Lisette onstage to the Merlin in character onstage, etc.—is often
so ambivalent as to make it nearly impossible to distinguish between the fictional and the real series of exchanges. When Lisette
in character calls Merlin in character an impertinent fellow,
Merlin, "interrupting the scene," replies, "Lisette, you're insult-
ing me right from the beginning of the scene; where will you end
up?"

> LISETTE: Oh, don't expect anything regular from me—I say
> what comes to me; let us go on.

MERLIN: Where are we?

LISETTE: I was treating your language as impertinent.

MERLIN: Say, you are in a bad mood; let's get on our way; let's not talk any more.

When Lisette in character insults Colette, the latter, sitting off-stage as a spectator since she is not supposed to appear in the scene, interrupts with: "Oh, yes: but is it acting to insult me in my absence?" When Colette in character is declaring her love for Merlin, the latter, "interrupting," cautions, "gently, Lisette, it is not decent to declare yourself so quickly." Stage direction or lover's caution? That is the question. In this exchange not only does the spectator of Marivaux's play lack the revealing (to the reader) "interrupting," but for him as for Blaise and Lisette there is no theatrical expression (*scène, jeu*) to permit a formal construction of the ambiguous phrase.

These ambiguities prove too much for Blaise and Lisette. When Colette onstage asks Merlin onstage if he would like to have her for a wife, Lisette attempts to cut through this false pretense:

MERLIN: I'd be delighted; but we'll have to be careful because of Lisette, whose meanness would be harmful and would hurt our plans.

COLETTE: If she weren't here, I'd know how to set us up; we should not have let her listen to us.

LISETTE: (*rising to interrupt*) What does that mean that I've just heard? 'Cause, after all, there's a speech which can't be part of your scene since I won't be present when you play it.

(scene iii)

And when Blaise, who has already found his mistress too eager to rehearse with Merlin *alone,* enters onstage, he has lost whatever capacity for objectivity he possessed. His warning to Merlin to stay away from Colette because she is to be his wife in one week is made in perfect good faith, but it provokes from the offstage Colette the announcement that she has decided to postpone the wedding still another week, and then, she "will see." Merlin's attempts after this to continue the rehearsal are futile. Blaise tells Lisette that the "comedy" was thought up only in order to leave them in the lurch, a comment which moves Colette to announce that, very well, she will jilt Blaise and since Merlin wants no more of Lisette, she and Merlin might just as well get married. When Merlin makes no denial of this, Lisette angrily tears up a piece of paper in token of her feelings for Merlin's comedy as well as of her feelings for him.

Apparently, in this first impromptu of *Les Acteurs*, we have an example of the use of the play as stratagem familiar in the century: the transformation of the formal, autonomous fiction into the real; the parallelism which is destroyed. For Merlin's fiction is apparently autonomous: Blaise and Lisette do know beforehand that they are dealing with a play, with make-believe, as docs not, for example, Mme Argante in the latter part of *Les Acteurs*. The breakdown of the formal into the informal occurs frequently, it is true, giving the impression of an interweaving pattern, but apparently this is not the true pattern, since after each breakdown Merlin attempts to re-establish the parallelism. It is as if Merlin (or Marivaux) had simply accelerated the possibility for these breakdowns by choosing as the basis for the autonomous fiction the real emotional relationships of the actors (who also retain their real names). The actors of Merlin's fiction are presumed to be acting even by the theater audience of the entire play—but are they? As for the second impromptu in *Les Acteurs*, the one put on by Mme Amelin with the help of the young widow Araminte, the theater audience is quite sure (as the onstage audience is not) that they are seeing a play, albeit one "which is being made up as it goes along." The language of this second impromptu, like that of the first, is double-edged, but, unlike that of the first, is not confusing to the audience of Marivaux's play.

The two impromptus are apparently the reverse of one another: in Merlin's, the formal breaks down into the informal; in Mme Amelin's, the informal is assimilated into the formal. Yet I must insist on the apparency of these distinctions, for a closer analysis shows both impromptus to be of the latter type: in each there is an a posteriori formalization of the informal, for the informal was clearly intended to make up in all its sincerity a part of the play being put on. Blaise and Lisette have been victimized in exactly the same way as Mme Argante: they have responded with real feeling to a false situation. Obscured though it is by Mme Ar-

gante's untimely arrival, the *entire rehearsal* is Merlin's impromptu. The real exchanges as well as the false or avowedly
fictional exchanges make up his comedy. Merlin counts on the
breakdown of the formal into the informal as the basis of his illusion. His impromptu is actually uninterrupted from the moment the actors enter onstage in scene iii until Blaise and Lisette
leave the rehearsal in a huff at the approach of Mme Argante in
scene v. Though Marivaux's spectator may have forgotten (as he
was expected to in the crisscross of ambiguities) which exchanges
make up the offstage and which the onstage action, Merlin and
Colette have been acting all the time. The alert spectator has probably caught on to this fact from even so small a clue as:

> COLETTE (*rising and interrupting*): Oh! *without interrupt-
> ing you,* that's put off to two weeks from Tuesday; between
> now and then, I'll see what happens.   (scene v)

But that they have been pretending all along becomes unmistaka-
bly clear at the end of scene v:

> COLETTE: We'll see each other later, eh, Monsieur Merlin?
> MERLIN: Yes, Colette, and it is going marvelously; these
> people love us, but let's still go on with our pretense.
> COLETTE: As much as you wish; there is no danger, since
> they love us so much.

Merlin's impromptu actually anticipates the pattern of Mme
Amelin's: just as Blaise and Lisette are actors in spite of themselves, so Mme Argante is to be both actor and spectator in spite
of herself. The informal is assimilated into the formal. But, in the
case of the valet's impromptu, the informal which is thus assimilated itself contains a formal element, Merlin's fiction about
himself and Colette which he actually counts on breaking down.
The play as stratagem is the substance of Merlin's little impromptu; Merlin is the author of a play within a play. And so,
too, is Mme Amelin, for when Blaise and Merlin do finally begin
playing (resuming at the point at which the rehearsal broke off),
they are presenting their play with its inner play within Mme
Amelin's impromptu. This time Mme Argante knows, naturally
enough, that she is watching a play, for she has suddenly ordered
the replaying of Merlin's little play in an effort to assuage the

insulted Mme Amelin. But Mme Argante does not know that she
is also acting in a play, for Mme Amelin's anger is all pretense,
part of the "revenge play" she is exacting of her friend. Thus the
structure of *Les Acteurs* is the most involved we have encountered: a play within a play within a play within a play.

The success of Merlin's impromptu, like that of Mme Amelin's,
depends on the *bonne foi* of the actors. Does this mean that, on
the question of the actor's art, Marivaux's position is exactly the
opposite of Diderot's first debater (whose position is usually attributed to Diderot)? For the latter, "sensibility is hardly ever the
quality of great genius." [2] Yet, even granting that such is Diderot's
position (his cautious position, for observe the modifying
"hardly"), Marivaux's is not necessarily opposite. For if the success of the impromptus in *Les Acteurs de bonne foi* depends on
the sincere feelings of Blaise and Lisette and Mme Argante, it
depends as well on the insincere feeling, the bad faith, of Merlin
and Colette and Mme Amelin. Like Diderot's *Paradoxe sur le
comédien,* Marivaux's little play is a debate about two different
esthetics, a presentation of two basically different theories of acting. In each debate there is no clear-cut victory for either of the
dramatically simplified positions (though it is delightfully ironic
in Diderot that the debater who speaks with the greatest feeling
is the opponent of feeling in art). The scope of Marivaux's debate
is even wider than Diderot's, for it opens up the question of the
actor's social status and of his native intelligence. After all, it
might be argued, Marivaux is apparently on the side of Diderot's
first debater, since Blaise is incapable of objectivity simply because he is an unintelligent peasant. Marivaux is making fun of
him. But this is to forget that the play also fools Lisette, a person
of a certain breeding (she is *suivante* to Angélique) and of real
insight into the objective nature of a play, as her objection to
many of the lines indicates (see, for example, the passage cited
above, p. 79). On the other hand, Colette, the daughter of the
gardener and herself a peasant in love with a peasant, is capable
of a degree of dramatic objectivity which even Mme Amelin might
envy. The effect of these characterizations is not to cancel out both
positions presented in Diderot's debate in their most extreme
forms, but rather to present each position in all its complexity.
For the complexity of the question is great. Even Merlin, one of

the actors in "bad faith," finds himself an actor in spite of himself, hence an actor in good faith. When he and Blaise do finally begin playing his own little play, it falls within Mme Amelin's little play—of which he knows nothing. The fooler fooled acts in good faith even while acting in bad faith.

"*Marivaudage!*—all that," snaps the confused, irritated spectator. An elaborate conceit, a clever and meaningless manipulation of ambiguities and paradoxes, a sterile intellectual structure of Chinese boxes, a miniature hall of mirrors in which even ceiling and floor are mirrors.

But no, for it is typical of Marivaux that the form which the inner play takes is an impromptu. *La Surprise de l'amour, La Double Inconstance, Le Jeu de l'amour et du hasard, L'Epreuve*— are these not all impromptus, plays in which the actors are left to their own wits once they are given the basic situation? This is the significance of the impromptu for Marivaux: it is a combination of the fixed and the moving, of bad faith and good faith. The given and the artificial make up the game of skill which is one moment of a Marivaux comedy: Merlin feigns love for Colette, Mme Amelin feigns dissatisfaction with Mme Argante. The moving and the sincere make up the game of chance which is the other moment of a Marivaux comedy: the jealousy of Blaise and Lisette, the consternation of Mme Argante.

Such, someone suggests, are the moments of the traditional comedia dell'arte, the ultimate in the impromptu form. But because Marivaux, like Pirandello, favors in this combination the play of chance, his theater cannot be so readily captured in this "influence." The sincere and the moving on which Marivaux and Pirandello rely is not itself a theatrical convention: a stock of well-rehearsed responses in the form of *lazzi* or portions of dialogue.[3] They rely rather on the sincerity of life itself. But because this sincerity, this living movement, is not itself without shape, their plays are not without shape. There is a limit or convention in life itself, and for both Pirandello and Marivaux this convention is found in the life of feeling. For the modern playwright, however, feeling means passion, and the shape which passion brings to life is a tragic one. Pirandello, in Fergusson's trenchant phrase, "sees human life itself as theatrical, as aiming at, and only to be realized in, the tragic epiphany." [4] It is because he would

violate this realization by his "skips" and "cuts," by having a man
die "at the wave of a baton," that the director in *Questa sera si
recita a soggetto* is chased from his own stage:

> THE CHARACTER ACTRESS: When you live a great passion,
> there you have true theater; and then the devil with a play-
> bill.
> THE LEADING LADY: You cannot play with passion!
> THE LEADING MAN: Manipulate everything just for an ef-
> fect, that's something you can do only with puppets.
> ALL THE OTHERS: On your way! On your way!
> DOCTOR HINKFUSS: But I am your director!
> THE LEADING MAN: No one can direct the birth of life!
>
> (Act III)

However, it is at this juncture that Marivaux and Pirandello part
ways. The feeling which *le hasard* or the sincere brings to modify
the fixed convention of the game in Marivaux is not passion but
sentiment, not *l'amour-passion* which issues in tragedy, but
l'amour-tendresse, which issues in comedy. Nor is this sentiment
a pallid substitute for passion, a playing of the major key in minor.
Marivaux does not give us pathos; he is not a Racine *à mi-chemin*.
His is a comic, not a tragic, sensibility.

Of course, there is more than this to distinguish the "life which
takes the stage" in Marivaux from that which does so in Pirandello.
The Italian dramatist's characters have no doubts about their
reality: it is because Hinkfuss would destroy their deeply felt
sense of the reality of the characters they are to portray that the
actors throw him out of the theater. The leading man tells the
director that under his own name he no longer exists, that he
must live, must be Rico Verri. The real issue in Pirandello is
not the ambiguity, not the interpenetration of true reality and
feigned reality, but the complex relationship of the real thing to
an artistic edition of it. The play within a play in Pirandello is
used to demonstrate the insufficiency of the "well-made play" to
grasp reality. Pirandello's actors know very well the true from the
false, life from art—and they know the difference before the play
begins. As Marivaux's actors do not. Marivaux is closer to Anouilh
(of *La Répétition,* for example) than he is to Pirandello. Yet, unlike Anouilh's actors, Marivaux's can tell the difference between

comedy and reality—but *after the fact*. Argante believes it when Mme Amelin says she was "only pretending"; Lisette accepts Merlin's designation of the play as play.

They can accept this post facto designation as true and not as simply another disguise in a never ending comedy, because there is a center to reality, or, in Pascalian terms, "une règle." Though Pascal despairs of ever being able to distinguish between feeling and fantasy and "a reason pliable in all directions," Marivaux does not. And it is perhaps a measure of his distance from the seventeenth century that the règle he chooses is not *raison* (however numerous the affective resonances of that term in the seventeenth century) but *feeling*. As Descartes in his search for epistemological certainty found "les premières notions," so Marivaux in his search for emotional certainty finds what might be called "les premiers sentiments." If in the game of skill which is the pretended love of a countess for a Lélio (*La Surprise de l'amour*) or of a Flaminia for an Arlequin (*La Double Inconstance*) the tools of the game are too slippery to control, if the player's skill is caught up in the player's pride—there need be no alarm; the change which chance (or life) has wrought can only be for the good. Les premiers sentiments can no more be wrong than Descartes's "clear and distinct ideas." Reality for Marivaux is an act of faith.

In *Les Acteurs de bonne foi* the actors—all of them—have been acting in good faith. Merlin and Colette, Mme Amelin and Mme Araminte undo the damage they have done by confessing that all was in jest. A cruel jest, perhaps (the cruelty of many of Marivaux's plays, of *L'Epreuve* in particular, has disaffected many critics), but this only makes the sense of relief all the greater. Merlin has always loved Lisette, Colette has never been unfaithful to Blaise, Mme Amelin has never ceased in her friendship for Mme Argante. Their "bad faith" was the false bad faith of the esthetic act, the double negative being necessarily based upon the positive good faith of actual feeling. Mme Amelin's stratagem was designed to gain nothing more than itself; the purpose of playing is playing. In *Les Acteurs de bonne foi* a real marriage contract is introduced not to frustrate but to please the victim.

The principle of dissociation is ultimately maintained. As with Corneille, the reality of the fictional has been only seeming. Like

Alcandre, Merlin (a familiar name for a trickster) concludes his play with a saving "ne . . . que." This restoration of distinction between play and reality is a characteristic and appropriate aspect of Marivaux dramaturgy. For equally as important as movement in a Marivaux comedy is the rest to which the movement comes. The revelation that all has been only comedy does not express a careless impatience on the part of the playwright to be done with his play once he has worked out his intricate pattern of confusion compounded by confusion. The revelation expresses rather the coincidence of good faith and chance necessary to prevent things from turning *au noir*. Movement, not for its own sake but toward stability—this is the structure of a Marivaux play. For all his sense of becoming, Marivaux is not our contemporary but stands rather as a transitional figure. In his feeling for the dynamics of feeling Marivaux is close to us, it is true; he is especially so in his feeling for the ambiguous, the "interpenetration of feigned reality and true reality." But in his feeling for the stable, for the rest to which movement comes, he is closer to the seventeenth century than he is to ours.

Nevertheless, useful as it is for definition, it is an injustice to Marivaux to locate him only relatively. For all his uniqueness in the eighteenth century, he is still fundamentally a man of that century. If in his awareness of ambiguity and complexity he transcends the literal-minded, propagandistic theater of the period, he is still a fully social-conscious dramatist. But he offers no drastic solutions nor is he even concerned with solutions, nor, more significantly still, with the social problems they are intended to solve. His social consciousness is deeper, providing not an answer to society's problems but an examination of society's premises. He examines not the obligations of the social contract on which society is based, but the bases of the contract itself; like all great artists, he is concerned with the sense of reality. Society is a game and like any other game the player must feel confident that none of his fellow players (or fellow citizens) is cheating, for society is based on the good faith of its members. Marivaux pushes the inquiry deeper than the casual acceptance of this commonplace. He seeks an assumption underlying even this one and he finds it in the belief in the goodness of the feelings. It is this more basic act of faith, indeed, which enables a Merlin to play with Lisette's feelings, or which prompts a Dorante (*Les Fausses Confidences*) to consent to Dubois's stratagem. In the midst of the confusion which this stratagem has wrought, Dorante exclaims: "In everything that happens here, Araminte, there is nothing true except my passion, which is infinite, and the portrait which I have made" (III.xii). Nothing more than Dorante's final stratagem, one says? No matter, for it, too is prompted by his sincere love. Yet we have no more reason to suspect this gesture of sincerity than does Araminte who is, in fact, charmed by it: "After all [she tells Dorante], since you truly do love me, what you have done to win my heart is not blamable; a lover has the right to find the right way to please, and one must forgive him when he has succeeded" (III.xiii). How could he fail to succeed, prompted as he is by the good faith which prompts all of the actors of "Le Théâtre de Marivaux, ou les acteurs de bonne foi"?

Chapter 7. Legouvé, Dumas, and Sartre

I. Legouvé and Dumas. The Play as Confessional

> Is it not monstrous that this player here
> But in a fiction, in a dream of passion,
> Could force his soul so to his own conceit . . .
> *Hamlet* (II.ii)

MARIVAUX is in direct line with all of the playwrights considered thus far: the focus of attention is the play or action and not the player or actor. The backstage or offstage interest (the emotions of Blaise and Lisette, for example) is not in and for itself, but looks to the play which is to be presented. Even in Corneille's *L'Il-lusion*, the evocation of Clindor's successive "careers"—including the central episode of his servitude to Matamore—can be seen as a dramatic preparation not only in the loose sense of teasing the emotions of the spectator but also as the dramatic preparation, strictly speaking, by Clindor for the career of actor. I have already suggested that this is historically true (the actor of the period was usually a jack-of-all-trades), but it can also be seen to be psychologically true according to what a modern esthetician of the theater has called the actor's "psychological readiness." [1] The multiplicity of careers prepares Clindor for a multiplicity of roles. Thus even here, where the emphasis seems to be on the actor rather than the action, it is so only with a view to finally presenting the actor acting; his offstage personality as such has little meaning except as it moves us closer to the stage. So, too, in Rotrou's *Saint Genest*, the play is the thing: through it the actor is converted, through it he gains an awareness of the more important play in which he is acting. Finally, in Molière's *Impromptu* we have observed the direct exclusion of interest in the artist offstage for the sake of concentrating interest on the artist onstage.

Beyond Marivaux old conceptions of the play do persist, of

course—the play as game and the play as stratagem, in particular —but only sporadically. For a new conception begins to emerge in the declining years of the eighteenth century, one which becomes increasingly dominant in the next century. The artist as a man, his personality for its own sake, becomes the focus of interest in those plays concerned with the theater. This interest, to be sure, had always existed: the backstage play was a particular favorite of the seventeenth century. There is now, however, a shift of emphasis: the outer play is not merely a kind of prologue to the central action of the play which the actors are to put on, but is itself the central action. If anything, the play within a play figures at best merely as an episode of the outer play. As interest shifts from the action to the actor, we go not only backstage with the man but offstage with him. In play after play about actors, either we do not see the hero onstage, or, when there is a play within a play, it is used only incidentally as a means of completing the impression of the man being drawn in the primary play. The play is conceived of not as a game or as a stratagem, not as a miracle and least of all as a mask—it is a portrait.

Ironically, one of the favorite subjects of this new emphasis on the man rather than the work is Molière. A recent bibliography of French plays in the period 1800–30 records no less than thirteen plays which, on the basis of title alone, have Molière as their subject.[2] The interest in the great comedian, however, is even older. Louis Sébastien Mercier's *Molière* dates from 1776 and anticipates the attempt of most of the later plays mentioned to portray the man in his private life rather than the artist in his professional life. The play is a grab-bag of events and personal relationships drawn from Molière's life and legend: his relations with his wife, the cabal around *Tartuffe,* his dealings with servants and friends. Molière is portrayed as a man who sacrifices serenity and security to the public good, his plays being considered didactic instruments aimed at correcting vice and elevating public morals. He is shown surrounded by shrewd servants, uncompromising enemies, and importunate friends from whom he seeks refuge only in Isabelle's love—where he finds only more disappointment. The brief inner play scene which occurs underscores negatively, as it were, that Mercier would rather talk about Molière as a dramatist than show him as one: Molière, who has been with Isabelle without the knowledge of Madeleine, has the girl suddenly begin rehearsing a scene from *Tartuffe* (Orgon's announcement to Marianne that he has destined her for the hypocrite) in order to make Madeleine, who has happened upon the lovers, believe that they were together for professional, not personal, reasons. The play is here a stratagem, but is so not through its content but by its form alone; the play within a play is related only externally to the primary action. There is some wit in the coincidence of Madeleine's entrance with the mention of Tartuffe's name, but, though deliberate, the wit is only incidental, another aspect of the portrait being drawn.

When the inner play is used as an integral moment of the intrigue, it is usually significant not in its substance but in the external occasion. If any positive conception of the play prevails in the portrait plays considered thus far, it is that of the play as stratagem (Molière's stratagem against Madeleine, for example, in Mercier's *Molière*). Now it is the essence of the play as stratagem to be concerned with an end beyond itself: the play is used for the accomplishment of some purpose in the real or offstage world which cannot be effected by direct action. Two actions are therefore developed in a temporal parallel until that moment most propitious for the effecting of the real purpose, when the parallel actions are suddenly made to converge. In the nineteenth century, as a consequence of the increased interest in the personality of the artist, this parallelism-plus-convergence formula gives way to a more radical fusion of the onstage and the offstage. The two realms meet each other not at the conclusion of the play within a play but at its beginning, as the man and the artist, the player and the role become one. The play is intended not to effect but to affect, not to implement an action but to express a being. The play becomes a confessional.

In Scribe's and Legouvé's *Adrienne Lecouvreur* (1849), the famous eighteenth-century actress whose burial in unconsecrated ground prompted Voltaire to a celebrated verse protest, the artist's subjective approach to art is typical of this confessional conception. The Princess de Bouillon, jealous of her lover, Maurice de Saxe, asks her confidant, the Abbé de Chazeuil, to discover the identity of Maurice's new mistress. To this end the abbé uses the princess' doltish husband, who, not knowing for whom the information is intended, says he can get it out of his own mistress, the actress Duclos. The latter is actually in the pay of the princess anyhow, so the princess sends her a note telling the actress that she wants to use the country place where the prince and Duclos usually tryst for a secret rendezvous with Maurice. At the theater, where the prince has gone to see Duclos on his mission, we switch backstage where we see Quinault, Poisson, and other actors preparing to go onstage in Racine's *Bajazet*. Adrienne, who is to play Roxane, enters, rehearsing some of her lines, just as the visiting Prince de Bouillon learns about a supposed infidelity in the form of a letter from his mistress Duclos to a supposed lover (actually the princess' note about the trysting place which was to be transmitted to Maurice). The backstage is left to Adrienne and Michonnet, the *régisseur*, as the actors go on to begin the play and the prince goes off to confirm the report about Duclos's infidelity. Adrienne reveals to Michonnet that she is in love with a certain young officer, but does not give his name. The revelation crushes Michonnet, himself in love with her. He leaves and Maurice enters. In a playful scene he and Adrienne declare their love for one another and promise to meet after the performance. When Adrienne goes onstage for her performance, the prince returns with the "letter from Duclos to Maurice," which he unwittingly sends to its original destinee, since the prince wishes to entrap Maurice in his rendezvous with the supposedly unfaithful mistress. Maurice, knowing who is the real author of the note, the princess to whom he is indebted for political reasons, comes backstage seeking a means of informing Adrienne that he will be forced to break their own rendezvous. He hits upon the device of writing his message on the blank scroll used as a stage prop for *Bajazet* in the fifth scene of the fourth act, in which Roxane receives Bajazet's intercepted letter to Atalide. When Adrienne reads the scroll with its real message, she is so upset that the audience is irrepressibly moved to applaud her "great acting." The second act of *Adrienne* ends with the actress, presumed to be offstage between the fourth and fifth acts of Racine's play, accepting the invitation to attend the little party which the prince is preparing for Maurice and Duclos.

It is unnecessary beyond this point to follow in strict detail the action of the play. We shall have occasion to cite later scenes of the play, but already we obviously have a clear instance of the confessional conception informing the play. We observe the conception, curiously enough, through a play outside the play, through the use of *Bajazet* which we never actually see performed by Adrienne and the other actors. (*Bajazet*, by the way, is presumed to run through four of its five acts in less time than it takes Scribe's second act to run its course—from II.iii to II.x!) We are nevertheless proxy spectators of Racine's play through the reactions of Michonnet in the wings. As Adrienne receives the prop letter which we know to contain a real message,

> MICHONNET (*looking to the left, toward the "stage"*): Zatime is coming on . . . Good! she doesn't have the letter . . . Yes . . . yes . . . she has it . . . she is giving it to Roxane . . . Lord! what an effect! . . . she shuddered . . . she can hardly stand up! her emotion is so strong that, in reading the letter, her make-up has fallen from her face. It's admirable (*vigorous applause*) Yes . . . yes . . . clap your hands . . . bravo! bravo! that's it! sublime . . . admirable!   (II.ix)

Through our proxy, then, this play outside the play becomes properly a play within a play, one in which Adrienne is depicted for us through her role. First of all, the identification is made in the most external fashion, through the similarity of the respective situations of Roxane and Adrienne: Adrienne is stunned by the letter from Maurice which cancels their rendezvous and which she interprets as a sign of betrayal even as Roxane is stunned by the letter of Bajazet in which she is betrayed. The letter, a tangible symbol of the oneness of Roxane and Adrienne, identifies both as women who deluded themselves about the sincerity of their beloved. Adrienne, it is true, is wrong about Maurice as Roxane is not about Bajazet, who really loves Atalide. But Adrienne's belief that she is as wronged as Roxane accounts for the sincerity of her acting, for her completely accurate rendition of the appropriate emotion in the letter scene. If there is apparently some contradiction in the fact that this joyful Adrienne has been called upon to play the jealous and outraged Roxane, we can perhaps fully appreciate the significance of Legouvé's and Scribe's choice of *Bajazet* as their inner play when we recall that it *is* joy which Roxane for the most part feels before she discovers Bajazet's treachery. Thus, the choice of *Bajazet* as the inner play in *Adrienne Le-*

couvreur is not to be considered as ironic or inconsistent but, if anything, prophetic. At every moment of the action Adrienne is superb not through artifice but through sincerity.

The language of plays serves as a channel for the actress' own feelings—offstage as well as on. Hearing Adrienne recount to Michonnet her first meeting with her unknown lover, we sense in Adrienne, as she invokes Corneille, that theatricalism, that invasion of life by the stage which we encountered as a temptation in Corneille himself. Maurice, it seems, came across four young blades who had accosted Adrienne with the most ignoble of intentions. As he leaped to her defense, Adrienne believed she heard:

Paraissez, Navarrois, Maures et Castillans
Et tout ce que l'Espagne a produit de vaillants! (*Le Cid,* v.i)

("Come forth, ye Navarrois, Moors, and Castilians, and all those valiant ones whom Spain has produced.")

and as he drove off the assailants one by one, Adrienne assures Michonnet,

[Et] le combat finit faute de combattants! (*Le Cid,* iv.iii) [3]

("And the battle finished for want of combatants!")

Adrienne constantly extends her esthetic of self-expression to all of art. Comparing herself and Maurice to La Fontaine's fable of *Les Deux Pigeons,* she chides her lover for seeing in the poem "only a fable." Much of this is lovers' banter, of course, but beneath the bantering tone of the woman in love lies once again the serious conception of art as personal expression.

In the moments of great crisis in her life, it is to the stage that Adrienne turns as a vehicle for the expression of her deepest feelings and her highest aspirations. Believing herself to have been betrayed by Maurice, she once more invokes the great Corneille to explain why she has nonetheless sacrificed her fortune to this "traitor":

Think! think, my friend, . . . if he owed it to me . . . if he had it from my hands! King by the tender care of her whom he abandoned and betrayed . . . King thanks to the devotion of the poor actress! Ah! he will try in vain, he will

not be able to forget me! If not his love, his very glory and
even his power will speak to him of me. Can you understand
now the meaning of my revenge?

"Crowned by my rewards, I want to overwhelm him with
them!" [4]

O, my revered Corneille, come to my aid! come sustain my
courage with these noble flights, with these sublime sentiments which you have so often placed on my lips. Prove to
them all that we who interpret your genius know how to
benefit from the contact with your great thoughts . . . get
something more than simply translating them well . . .
(IV.iv)

And in the crashing scene which concludes Act IV, convinced that
she has not only been jilted by Maurice for the princess but also
insulted by his refusal to acknowledge the sacrifice of her fortune
in his behalf, Adrienne turns once more to the stage, to Phèdre's
self-flagellation as her young stepson refuses her. Turning first to
Maurice and then to the princess, the overwrought actress recites
from *Phèdre:*

> Pourrait-il contenir l'horreur qu'il a pour moi?
> Il se tairait en vain! je sais mes perfidies,
> Oenone, et ne suis point de ces femmes hardies . . .
> Qui, goûtant dans le crime une honteuse paix,
> Ont su se faire un front qui ne rougit jamais! . . .[5]
> (*Phèdre*, III.iii; *Adrienne Lecouvreur*, IV.ix)

(Can he contain the horror he feels for me? He will be silent
in vain. I know my perfidies, Oenone, and I am not one of
those bold women . . . who, savoring in crime a shameful
peace, have learned to show a brow which never blushes.)

Reciting these last verses, Adrienne makes her meaning unmistakable by pointing her accusing finger at the Princess de Bouillon.
Adrienne has decidedly little luck with Racine: two of his plays
have been for her occasions of Maurice's supposed treachery.
Finally, the dying Adrienne recalls that it was through certain
verses of Corneille's *Psyché* that she had hoped to express, for
the first time, her love to Maurice. She had even insisted on re-

storing this old work to the troupe's repertoire over the objections of her fellow actors precisely in order to be able to confess through its verses her love "in front of everyone without anybody suspecting it . . ." And as she passes into delirium, the dying actress does recite the verses in question (*Psyché*, III.iii.1065–77). But as her delirium continues, she turns to the other strong emotion her affair with Maurice had provoked: jealousy—also expressed through the verses of a play, through Hermione's warning to Pyrrhus in Racine's *Andromaque* (IV.v.1381 ff.).

Adrienne's is an existence imbued with the theater. Her very subconscious expresses itself in the precise verses of the classical dramatists; Cornelian heroic comedy and Racinian tragedy represent the poles of her nature. Yet, in spite of the evident sincerity of Adrienne's theatrical allusions, the impression which the confessional of *Adrienne Lecouvreur* leaves us with is not that the actress is expressing herself through the theater, but that the theater is expressing itself through the actress. Life does not invade the stage; the stage invades life. Adrienne's relationship to the theater is passive; she stands back from it for a moment, as it were, asking it to help her in her life's struggles—as, for example, in her invocation to Corneille. If it is herself she truly expresses through the channel of the theater, then we must conclude that a very theatrical self is the essence of Adrienne. Ultimately we shall have to come to the same conclusion about Dumas's actor, Kean. The road to the conclusion there, however, is more devious. Let us follow it.

The fact that Kean is an actor is paradoxically almost forgotten in Dumas's play.[6] Kean is formally onstage for only a relatively short period. We are more often physically offstage with him: in Act I we see him in high society, at the home of Eléna; in Act II in his private lodgings; in Act III in low society, at the sailors' inn; in Act IV backstage at the Drury Lane Theater, receiving those people who make up his offstage world; in Act V at home once again, settling his complicated relationship to Anna Damby and Eléna. Even in the play within a play—the balcony scene from *Romeo and Juliet*—Kean seems to be onstage only to come off it. Kean is a dandy, a lover, a cavalier, a man of the world, a counselor to young girls—everything but an actor.

Yet Kean is all of these things as an actor. In fact, when he is
acting, it is only to the extent that he is these things, severally or
individually, that he is a good actor. For Kean's theory of acting
is based not on observation but on self-expression (I shall later
consider the more complex theory of self-observation). At the
heart of Kean's esthetic lies that subjectivity which some have
seen as the very essence of romanticism.[7] There is no distinction
for Kean between the offstage and the onstage. Kean is the actor
who spends his free time in a search for authenticity of the feelings he will be called on to present in the theater. This search
for authenticity takes place in the company of fellow actors named
Bardolph, David, Tom—all Shakespearean actors who bear in offstage life not only the very names of the master's characters but
their namesakes' reputations as roisterers and low types. The curtain no longer separates illusion and reality.

Kean refuses to give up the emotions of the theater. Which
ones? Those which he experiences as he receives the applause (or
even the disapproval) of the audience, the emotions consequent
upon the exercise of his talents and hence emotions common to
all men in all professions—pride, satisfaction, etc.? Or those emotions identical with the exercise of his talents, the emotions of the
roles he fills? Kean's further defense of his profession before Lord
Mewill suggests that it is both, suggests indeed that the pride he
feels in the applause of the audience or the pain he feels in its
disapproval constitute for him a judgment not on his talent but
on his person. When Lord Mewill, who had appeared at the inn
masked in order to further his plot against Anna, has been un-
masked by Kean but refuses to duel with the actor because he
considers Kean a mere *saltimbanque,* the actor with heavy sarcasm
reminds him: (1) that Lord Mewill was born in his estate only to
squander his patrimony in debauchery, whereas Kean was born
"among the ruins of the populace" and has made for himself "a
name the equal of the noblest"; (2) that Mewill wanted to re-
establish his fortune by a heartless marriage to a young girl who
did not want him, whereas Kean, the lowly actor, "offered refuge
to the fugitive"; (3) that Mewill, a peer of the realm, goes skulk-
ing about in a mask, using another's name, whereas the actor
Kean goes about under his own name and "his face fully uncov-
ered." Not for Kean the popular conception of the actor as a liar,

of the theater as illusion. It is Kean's special pleasure, in fact, to demonstrate in his reproaches to Mewill that quite the reverse is true: the world is a lie and the theater truth. The most telling proof of this reversal of the popular view is Mewill's mask, the traditional symbol of the fictitious and the false—"whereas the actor Kean rips off the mask of every face, in the theater as well as the tavern." Does Kean simply have in mind that cliché about the theater as the exposer of duplicity (think of *Tartuffe,* for example)? Possibly: that the theater should be conceived of as a means of getting at essential truth is not inconsistent with the esthetic of sincerity which Kean bespeaks. However, Kean's reproach to Mewill is less objective than subjective, directing our interest not to the play as an expression of society but to the player as an expression of himself. Kean "rips the mask from every face," including his own. Kean does not become Hamlet; Hamlet becomes Kean.

Or Othello becomes Kean, as in the actor's backstage rendezvous with Eléna. The latter, more thrilled by than anxious about Kean's jealousy, calls the actor "mon Othello"—a characterization which Kean answers to by calling Eléna "Desdemona." And it is because he feels like Othello when he is expected to play Romeo that Kean appeals to the Prince de Galles to give up Eléna:

> If I said to your Highness: We artists, milord, have strange love affairs, which resemble in no way those of other men; for they never cross the footlights; yet these loves are no less passionate and jealous. Sometimes it happens that from among the women who come habitually to our plays, we choose one whom we make the inspiring angel of our genius.
>
> (IV.vi)

Is it simply the *amour-propre* of the artist, the pride in his talent, and not the heart of the man which is touched? Is it simply the artistry of simulated feeling which is dedicated to the "ange inspirateur" even as the cobbler's apprentice might dedicate his craftmanship to his mistress? Hardly, for the man in this case is not separated from his talent: "All that our roles have of tenderness and passion, it is to her that we address it . . . The two thousand spectators in the theater disappear for our eyes which see

only her . . ." The passion is real, not simulated—so real as to
make the actor forget what, in his speech refusing to leave the
theater, seemed to be indispensable: the plaudits of the public:
"[They] are unimportant to us . . . it is not for reputation, for
glory, for the future that we act; it is for a sigh . . . a look . . .
a tear from her" (IV.vi).

Kean continues to speak of "acting." He has even based his
appeal to the prince on a distinction between the loves of other
men and the "amours bizarres" of artists which do not get beyond
the footlights. He reminds the prince that, thanks to his position
and his natural endowments, he can have almost any woman in
the real world he wants. The stage and the offstage, then—and the
distinction is made by Kean himself. But a real distinction? Or is
it not one that the actor hopes to create (or possibly only take
advantage of) in the prince's mind? When Kean calls his happiness ". . . vain et . . . frivole" he is only recognizing the prince's
probable judgment upon it, the judgment of the world of reality
on the world of dream. For his own part, the happiness which
this bizarre love brings "is nevertheless a form of happiness." It
is, indeed, his whole life, as he makes clear to the prince when the
latter charges him with being Eléna's real lover: "No milord! all
that I feel for her is this artist's love of which I have spoken to you,
to which the greatest actors have owed their greatest successes . . .
but this love . . . I have made it my life, you see . . . more than
my life: my glory; more than my glory: my happiness!" (IV.vi)
Through the opéra-impromptu of Le Malade imaginaire Cléante
made love to his fellow actress: two actions occurred simultane-
ously, one fictional, the other real. In Kean's onstage love-making
the onstage and the offstage constitute one unbroken plane of action as Kean makes love to a spectator.

For Kean is the actor who will not play the happy lover Romeo
(happy at least in the famous balcony scene) while his heart is
breaking. Kean's antiparadoxical esthetic of acting will not permit
him to make love to Eléna from onstage while his heart is seething
with jealousy over the discovery that the Prince de Galles makes
expensive gifts to her: "Oh! cursed profession! where no feeling
belongs to us, where we are masters neither of our joy nor of our
sorrow . . . where, the heart broken, one must play Falstaff; or,
the heart joyous, one must play Hamlet! Always a mask! never a
face!" (IV.viii) The public, he complains, "takes us for automatons

. . . having no other passions than those of our roles . . . I will not play" "Always a mask"—Kean is, of course, dramatizing his sense of frustration. From his own discussion of the "ange in-spirateur," with all its subjective implications, we can believe that he has played on occasions when the role was not a mask—those occasions, for example, which gave rise to the gossip reported to Eléna early in the play that he was playing directly to her. But here he is stating his esthetic negatively: as a matter of practical fact, an actor must on some occasions play those roles which do not suit him in either his fundamental nature or his mood of the moment. But, contrary to the ideal actor of Diderot's first de-bater, it would be on just those occasions that Kean would be least impressive. It is just such an external matter of fact which forces Kean on this occasion to do violence to his feelings, to play falsely: his old companions, the saltimbanques, depend on this benefit performance. Even so, when Kean goes out on the stage as Romeo even though his heart is breaking, those in the know are seeing something of the fundamental Kean: his loyalty and gen-erosity.

Onstage, however, the feelings for Eléna overcome those for the old friends. Loyalty and generosity carry him—imperfectly— through to the moment of farewell, but, climbing over the balus-trade of Juliette's balcony, Kean spies the prince in Eléna's box, so that instead of making his exit, the actor returns to the stage from which he stares at the prince and Eléna. Juliette and the prompter attempt to bring Kean back to his exit line, "Ma Juliette, adieu," but

> KEAN (*laughing*): Ah! Ah! Ah!
> SALOMON (*prompting*): Romeo!
> JULIETTE: Romeo!
> KEAN: Who calls me Romeo? Who believes that I am play-ing the role of Romeo here?
> JULIETTE: Kean, are you going mad?
> KEAN: I am not Romeo . . . I am Falstaff, the companion of the Crown Prince of England in his debaucheries . . .
>
> (IV.i)

Even Kean's irony is literal-minded: the alternative to the false conception of himself as Romeo is another theatrical conception of himself—Falstaff. His discovery of truth comes to him not in a

contrast between the stage and life, but in one between two stage
figures: he comes offstage as Romeo only to go onstage as Falstaff,
or, to accept his later refinement on the self-characterization, as
Polichinelle, "the Falstaff of the public squares." And Falstaff he
is now, even as in the backstage love scene with Eléna he was
Othello: the companion of the Prince of Wales only in merry-
making and debauch. Kean comes to that vision of himself which
Eléna's husband had invoked earlier when speaking of the actor's
expected appearance at a party the prince was to give: "In his
clown's role; we shall have him play a scene of Falstaff after dinner . . ." (I.iii).

So Kean on the stage of the Drury Lane rejects the role which
does not express his true self in order to identify himself in the
role which does. "Professional mania," one says? There is too much
evidence in *Kean* to suggest that it is more: personal mania. The
play within a play does not end with Kean's interruption of the
balcony scene; another one simply begins. Or the single play which
is Kean's whole existence simply goes on, as Kean, with the same
self-congratulatory pride he had shown toward the false Mewill
at the inn, generously forgives the false Eléna. For what does he
do thereby but repeat the lesson he had given Mewill: the actor,
the supposed professional liar, is the man of integrity, while the
noble-born Eléna, like the noble-born Mewill, goes about with a
false face. Offstage and onstage we have seen Kean playing himself. As he will no doubt continue to do in New York with Anna
Damby. For Kean the play is a confessional, a public platform
from which the essential Kean can reveal himself in all sincerity.
And perhaps nothing so clearly defines this particular conception
in Dumas's play as the counterconception which informs Jean-
Paul Sartre's adaptation of *Kean*.

II. Sartre. The Play as Lie

> COSTARD: *I Pompey am,—*
> BOYET: You lie, you are not he.
> *Love's Labour Lost* (v.ii)

Sartre has changed the play radically.[8] Accepting the basic story
line from Dumas, he has strongly modified the principal roles.
Anna Damby, for example, is not the naive creature of Dumas's

play but is rather a scheming little bourgeoise, quite capable of handling for herself the Mewills of this world and quite determined to have Kean as a husband. Eléna, too, is a different character: blasé, less flighty, much more the sardonic, self-possessed woman of the world as opposed to the somewhat girlishly fickle countess of Dumas. By far the most radical change, however, is in the character of Kean himself: Sartre's hero is ironic in his world-weariness, more destructive in his self-absorption than the starry-eyed Kean of Dumas. The Sartrean hero has a less exalted notion of his art, for he knows the play for what it is—no romantic identification with the role for him. Behind this Kean's ironical, self-castigating demeanor lies the conception of the theater as a vast deception and of the actor's life as a fabric of lies. This Kean's esthetic (if he may be said to have one at all) contains no idea of experiencing all the passions which are to be shown on the stage, for the actor, having no real self to expose to experience, has no real passions to present. Sartre has apparently delighted in a total reversal of the first Kean's conceptions and ideals.

Having no emotions to express, this Kean reverses the experience-expression relationship of Dumas's actor. He tells the prince: "My lord, I have therefore expressed all the passions; each morning I take one which I match with my suit and it lasts me all day long. Today I have chosen nobility" (i.v). The stage gives its emotions to him, not he his emotions to the stage. It is true that later, when he refuses to give up Eléna despite the fact that the Prince de Galles fears the affair will strain relations with Denmark, Kean does sound like the old version: "If England wishes to keep me, let her leave me my passions. I must have all of them in order to be able to express them all. I had 'til now experienced only the joys of love; now I know the anguish of love and you can measure the advantages of my experience if you come to see me play *Othello*" (ii.ii). But the emotions are to be experienced here prior to their representation not as an article of some well-articulated theory of acting, but only as an argument to enable Kean to keep Eléna. The actor's opportunism defines not only his lack of scruples but also his lack of a coherent esthetic.

Kean's only bearings are his love for Eléna, born more of defiance than of true affection, and his talent, the external and technical aspect of his profession. Feeble as it is, his talent is his

only moral guide, offstage as well as on. For the stage only mirrors
the lie of life. Everything, therefore, is to be treated as a play.
When Anna, who has come to Kean for advice about a stage
career, is not intimidated by his warnings, he becomes scornful of
the talents which the daughter of a cheese-maker might have (as
for the warnings, they are essentially those Dumas's actor gives,
but Sartre's actor gives them in a spirit not of solicitude but of
scorn). Anna rehearses—badly—Ophelia's mad scene, causing
Kean to sneer not only at her acting but at her wanting to act:

> You don't act in order to earn a living. You act in order to lie,
> to lie to yourself, to be what you cannot be and because you
> have had enough of being what you are. You act in order not
> to know yourself and because you know yourself too well.
> You play heroes because you are a coward and saints because
> you are a sinner; you play murderers because you have been
> dying to kill your neighbor, you act because you are a born
> liar. You act because you love the truth and because you hate
> the truth. You act because you would go crazy if you didn't.
> Act? Do I know when I am acting? Is there a moment when I
> stop acting?   (II.iii)

Everything is a lie—or a play. So Kean proposes that Anna prove
herself further in a rehearsal of the very situation in which they
find themselves: a young girl coming to the great actor for advice
about going on the stage; Kean is to play the actor who would se-
duce the girl. Believing that at the moment of surrender Anna
will not want to go through with her "part," Kean hopes to prove
once again the bluff, the illusionism of the world. But though she
momentarily weakens, Anna is quite willing to go through with
her part. As Kean is not with his. For Kean's "part" was to play a
part—not to take Anna in reality. Or was it? Kean does not really
know. Having hired Anna with a "sans conditions" which neither
he nor she is sure was part of their little comedy, he dismisses her.
Playing at playing offstage, Kean loses his bearings completely.
Onstage he will regain them, if only negatively. Knowing at least
that he is not Romeo, he, with his unslaked thirst for reality,
knows more than the imbecilic audience with its too easily slaked
thirst for falsity. Dumas's Kean hated the public because it could

not see the reality it was getting; Sartre's Kean hates it because it
cannot see the unreality it is getting.

When Sartre's Kean confronts Lord Mewill, there is no romantic
reversal of the stage-life relationship, no ironic contrast between
Mewill's real mask and Kean's stage mask. Indeed, when the Kean
of Sartre learns that Anna's "contact" at the inn will probably
be masked, he replies: "Masked? (*He begins to laugh.*) I have no
luck: I leave the world of the theater only to re-enter it. I have had
enough of the theater, I have, enough of swords, of mysteries, of
masked conspirators. Do you know why I am here? To eat and to
drink. That is really living. I have the right to live, don't I?"
(III.v) Unlike Dumas's hero, who tore the mask off every face, in
the theater as in the tavern, Sartre's actor accepts the mask as the
traditional symbol of the false world of the theater. Furthermore,
when Sartre's Kean begs the prince to give up Eléna, he brings
up no mysterious, subjective theory of an "ange inspirateur." It is
as a man that this Kean wants the woman (I have already com-
mented on the opportunism of his bargaining with the prince
when he argues that Eléna is necessary to his acting). And it is the
man, driven by his desire and his jealousy, not the artist in search
of authenticity among Shakespearean stage types, who spends a
night of debauch. Sartre's actor cares little about the material
sacrifices his art demands of him; he renounces art because it de-
prives him of self-hood. The Sartrean Kean is prepared, in a way
that Dumas's actor is not, to give up the stage. In Dumas's play
when Salomon reproaches the actor for the disorder which he sees
as the source of the actor's financial difficulties, Kean retorts: "Be
orderly! That's it! . . . and genius, what becomes of my genius
while I get more order in my ways?" (IV.ii) We recall that the subtitle of Dumas's play is *Désordre et génie*. The coordinating con-
junction is the appropriate one: *et*—that is, "equals," for Kean's
genius is his disorder, the free expression of his nature without the
artifices of order. Sartre's Kean, too, associates genius and disorder:
to Anna who has just proposed marriage as a stabilizing influence
in his disorderly life, Kean replies in romantic fashion: "Order!
That's it! and what becomes of my genius when I get order?"
(III.iv) But, as earlier in his plea to the prince to leave Eléna to
him, the romantic esthetic echoed here is used opportunistically

by Kean to counter Anna's proposal of marriage. The moment, as we shall see, comes when Sartre's Kean quite readily gives up his stage career, an unthinkable renunciation for Dumas's actor.

The modern Kean cares little about public recognition; he is too preoccupied with self-cognition. But his refusal to go onstage is buttressed by more immediate reasons as well: Eléna does not want Kean to go on if Anna is to play Desdemona in the *Othello* which is the play within a play of Sartre's adaptation. If Anna does go on, Eléna threatens to play up to the Prince de Galles while Kean is onstage, for she knows that this will probably drive the actor nearly insane and thus, she hopes, destroy his performance. Considering Kean's pride in his talent, the actor is thus open to the loss of the only two things he clings to: Eléna and his professional skill. So he does his best to replace Anna (who has replaced someone else) and, when he cannot, refuses to go on. It is only for the sake of the destitute saltimbanques that he finally relents, Eléna's threats notwithstanding. (This sentimentality for his old comrades is an aspect of Kean's character which Sartre has accepted from Dumas perhaps only to get his actor onstage.)

The Sartrean Kean goes on as Othello. It is almost as if Sartre wanted to underscore his actor's purely technical relationship to his art by making the parallel between the role and the actor as intimate as possible. For the outraged and jealous Othello appears to be the perfect role for the outraged and jealous Kean to play. But it is the very outrage he is feeling which threatens to *prevent* this Kean from playing Othello. Faltering at the sight of the prince with Eléna, this Kean is enabled to continue not through some parallel between his own emotions and those of the role but through the reawakening of what might be described as his professional emotions—those which would enable him to play the enraged Othello superbly but "cold." As Kean looks distractedly into Eléna's box, Lord Mewill hisses and it is these hisses which bring Kean back to "reality." Kean continues from this point "en Othello superbe"—but the heckling from Eléna and the prince becomes finally intolerable. As Eléna laughs when Kean-Othello begins to suffocate Anna-Desdemona, the actor stops the play and turns to Eléna's box to address the prince: "Where do you think you are? at court? in a boudoir? Everywhere else, you are prince, but here I am king and I am telling you that you are

going to be quiet right now or we will stop playing. We are working, Sir, and if there is anything that idlers ['oisifs'] should respect,
it is the work of others" (IV.5th tabl.ii).

As an actor Kean is king, but only when he is acting. He has no
"delusions of grandeur" that playing Othello or Hamlet makes
him king or prince. Indeed, the Sartrean Kean's external relationship to his roles brings him a peace Dumas's Kean could never
know: even as Falstaff, the Sartrean Kean would be king—in the
theater. This does not mean, however, that the Sartrean actor
would not give all to be Othello, or, for that matter, even Falstaff.
Having interrupted his playing with the bitter reminder to himself that he is fact not Othello, he pleads: "My God, let me be
Othello, give me his force and his rage!" (IV.5th tabl.ii). The
earlier Kean had also interrupted his playing because "he was not
his role," but he did so only to assume another role: Falstaff. The
modern Kean would accept this characterization of himself with
less rue. As it is,

> On this matter, I was wrong, a while ago, to speak to you
> of Kean. Kean died at an early age. (*Laughter.*) Shut up, you
> murderers, it is you who killed him. It is you who took a
> child in order to make of him a monster! (*Frightened silence
> of the public.*) That's it. Perfect: quiet, the silence of death.
> Why should you hiss: there is no one onstage. No one. Or
> perhaps an actor acting Kean in the role of Othello. Hold,
> there: I am going to confess something to you: I don't exist,
> I am only pretending. In order to please you, ladies and gen-
> tlemen, in order to please you. And I (*he hesitates and then
> with a gesture of "what's the use"*) . . . that's all.
>
> (IV.5th tabl.ii)

Dumas's actor, overcome with emotion, had to be carried offstage;
Sartre's actor, born into awareness, walks off "slowly, in the
silence."

Born into awareness: that, to recall the prince's earlier definition, "un acteur, c'est un mirage" (I.iv). Ironically, like the Kean
of Dumas, Sartre's actor ultimately identifies himself with his roles,
but with this crucial difference: that he confirms in their unreality
his own unreality. An actor does not exist, so that when, the following day, Salomon tells Kean that some actors have come

inquiring after his health, Kean replies: "Actors? Then there was no one. (*He laughs.*) No one! No one!" (v.ii) Having fled from reality as an actor, Kean, who had earlier wanted to "lean with his own weight upon the world," now cherishes the reality of self-hood. He would sooner go to jail than apologize to the prince, for if the authorities put him in prison, "it's because they take me for a man" (v.ii). He is through with his old existence as a *bouffon,* one in which, the man having been false, everything around him was false. He will wait for the police "in this armchair." You mean, Salomon corrects, "in the armchair of Richard III." No, Kean corrects in turn, "in *this* armchair." *This* is a real chair. The chair of Richard III does not exist; it belongs to the world of gestures. But, as Salomon reminds his master, Kean is still living in that world: waiting for the police in his chair, he is simply playing a scene from a play he has recently been considering. Says Kean, "You're right, damn it, I wanted to make a gesture. Do you know, I used to be filled with gestures: there were some for every hour of the day, for every season of the year, for every period of life. I had learned to walk, to breathe, to die. Fortunately, these gestures are now dead" (v.ii). Or these gestures are almost dead. It will, of course, be difficult to exorcise those that remain, but Kean's imitative talent will help him here: "It will come little by little. I shall imitate the natural until it becomes second nature" (v.ii). But it will not be Kean who will be going through these Pascalian paces; it will be "M. Edmond, jeweler."

One of Kean's gestures which still survives in M. Edmond is the passion for Eléna, a passion which will be exorcised only when she has forced him, in that typically Sartrean image, "au pied du mur." When Eléna comes to his place, Kean confronts her with his decision to abandon the stage as the first step in his quest for reality. He invites her to share this new existence (indeed, his first true existence) in which he will be jeweler, not actor. When Eléna at first refuses his invitation, Kean charges her with having until that moment merely played a role. Eléna takes up the challenge and Kean, as with Anna Damby earlier, now finds his fellow actress prepared to go further than he had expected: "Let us leave!" she suddenly urges. When Kean, even as with Anna, hesitates, Eléna lashes out at him for *his* play-acting. Eléna must repeat the lesson of the previous night before Kean can act: "Have no fear, sir: I give you back your freedom. You will flee alone, you will go alone to make a triumphant trip around the continent. Oh, don't think that I hold any grudge against you; on the contrary, it is I who should excuse myself. I was foolish enough to take you for a man and it is not your fault if you are only an actor" (v.vi). And an actor, Eléna quotes the prince to Kean, is only the reflection of a man. Kean does not ignore the lesson a second time; he attempts to carry off Eléna. In order to "show the prince"? Ultimately, yes, but for the moment to show up Eléna. He makes his show of force, fully realizing that she is not ready to respond to it. For the sake of M. Edmond, Kean is playing his last role, bringing the stage into life as a judgment upon the falsity of life and not, as with the Kean of Dumas, out of a sense of the superiority of the stage over life. Nor is Kean himself condemned in this overreaching judgment, for it touches only those idlers (*oisifs* or *salauds* in the more familiar existentialist vocabulary) who are prepared to love only the false. Eléna is a *oisive,* for she is unwilling to leave with Kean when the chips are really down. The prince is a *oisif,* for if the old Kean was but a reflection of a man, the prince, who lived as Kean's reflection, was doubly unreal: the reflection of a reflection. The old Kean, Eléna, the prince: "Three reflections: each of the three believing in the reality of the other two: that's the theater for you" (v.vi).

M. Edmond will have none of the theater. Eléna having been disposed of, Kean announces his intention to marry Anna and to accompany her to New York. When the prince discovers that Kean no longer loves Eléna, he, too, ceases loving her—thus confirming Kean's assessment of him as a reflection. When, robot-like, the prince becomes interested in Kean's new love, Anna, the latter tells him that Kean is only pretending to have forsaken Eléna— and, robot-like, the prince resumes his love for Eléna. The play ends with Kean's telling Salomon to reserve two places on the ship to New York only to have Salomon promise to reserve three: one for himself, for "from the moment that you put on a play, you two, you will need a prompter!" (v.xi)

Taken as more than a labored wisecrack, Salomon's remark makes explicit what seems to be implicit in Sartre's denouement: that Kean will resume his acting career in the States. To the

extent that this is true, Sartre's play suffers from an error of conception. For his hero has moved toward a rejection of the stage,
whereas Dumas's had moved toward an acceptance of it. The romantic Kean discovers that reality and value are to be found
only in the theater, the supposed world of make-believe and unreality. This is the meaning of his reproach to Mewill at the inn
and of his release of Eléna from her commitment to him. Sartre's
actor also discovers that the offstage world is only playing a comedy, but he does not turn to the stage to discover reality, for the
stage only mirrors the lie of life. He rejects both comedies. This is
an appropriately Sartrean concept: as the historian of *La Nausée*
rejects history, the illusion of discovering reality in the past, so
Sartre's actor rejects the theater, the illusion of discovering reality
in illusion itself. The theater is not a world of real choices, says
the disabused Kean, but only of make-believe choices. The actor
is not free; he is, to paraphrase Hamlet, illusion's slave.

Sartre's *Kean* is not, in the manner of the play from which it is
drawn, an *éloge de l'acteur;* it is rather a critique of the theater.
In the critique, apparently, the esthetic derived turns against the
play itself (one is reminded of the same paradox in Rotrou's *Saint
Genest*). Sartre is not unaware of the paradox: as much as it is
Kean who berates the imaginary audience of *Othello*, it is Pierre
Brasseur who berates the real audience of *Kean* with his taunt
that there is no one onstage, that he does not really exist, that
perhaps the audience is seeing an actor playing Kean playing
Othello. And no doubt Sartre is aware that according to the rejection of art his Kean proposes, his own play, as an adaptation
of an adaptation (de Courcy through Dumas through Sartre), is
worse even than the prince's love: a copy of a copy of a copy.

The Sartrean paradox is not irresolvable, however. The actor
does make real choices: to play Hamlet or Othello in this way or
that, to create his effect with this gesture or that, etc. The actor's
freedom, as Kean himself realized before the "illumination" which
canceled out even this perception, lies in the practice of his *métier.*
Moreover, we need not confuse Sartre with his actor: for one
thing, we remember that Sartre, like Pirandello, presents his
"rejection of art" within a work of art; for another, it is the
esthetician Sartre who replies to the Sartrean actor's view and
finds it wanting. In his thirst for reality, Sartre's Kean is incapable

of the duplicity which the Sartre of *Qu'est-ce que la littérature?* recognizes as essential to the esthetic act. We cite at random from the text:

> Thus the writer appeals to the freedom of the reader in order for him to collaborate in the creation of his work (p. 97).
>
> . . . . .
>
> Thus reading is an act of *generosity;* and what the writer asks of the reader is not the application of some abstract freedom, but the gift of his whole person, with his passions, his hesitancies, his sympathies, his temperament, his scale of values (p. 100).
>
> . . . . .
>
> Certainly I do not deny, when I read, that the author can be impassioned, nor even that he might have conceived the first idea of his work under the empire of passion. But his decision to write supposes that he withdraws ["prenne du recul"] from his emotions; in a word, that he transforms his emotion into free emotions, as I do with mine in reading him, that is, that he be in a posture of generosity (pp. 104–5).

The actor Kean is in the same situation before his roles as the reader before a text. But where Sartre's reader is expected to make a gift of his emotions to the text, Sartre's Kean prays that some of the passion of the role be given to him. (As the emphasis on "recul"—Sartre's version of the familiar "esthetic distance"—indicates, the similarity between Sartrean "generosity" and romantic subjectivity is only seeming.) Moreover, Kean wants these emotions as primary experiences, not transformed, as Sartre would have them, "en émotions libres." The actor lacks the necessary recul by which he would discover his freedom from as well as through the role.

Sartre's play, then, unlike Sartre's player, does not necessarily propose a rejection of all plays. If the imaginary Kean will not act in any more plays, this does not mean that his creator has to cease writing plays. Sartre has taken sufficient recul from his creation not to identify with it. Unlike his actor, the dramatist does not feel that he is running away from himself in the esthetic act.

Portrait and confessional: the man without the work or the man through the work. Whatever other interest may lie at the heart of the change in sensibility which has been fought over under the label of romanticism, an examination of the artist on-stage leads to the conclusion that it is in the personality of the hero, in his being more than his deeds, that the dramatists of the period are interested. Romantic subjectivity portends a special frustration for the dramatist or actor, for, as one student of romanticism has put it: "The theater is, or ought to be, an objective art, one where the artist as a person effaces himself before the characters whom he has act and speak; now, the romantic movement tends to the free and direct expression of temperament, of the feelings, of the ideas of the writer. There is, therefore, an essential incompatibility between the theater and romanticism." [9] So-called romantic drama reverses the Aristotelian formula that "tragedy is an imitation not of men, but of an action and of life, and life consists in action, not a quality." [10] The "action" of Dumas's *Kean,* for example, is to show the great actor from a series of different angles, with the unity of the piece being not the rather thin story of Kean's affair with the Countess Eléna, but the character of Kean himself. Hence the episodic structure of the play, with each episode bringing a new line to the portrait or highlighting a line already drawn. The portrayal of Kean's character—it is this conception of *Kean* which explains his seemingly too easy acceptance, in spite of all dramatic probability, of Eléna's rejections of him after he has suffered so much for her. This acceptance provides one more instance of Kean's superiority as a person over the well-born Eléna—just as the episode at the inn proved his superiority over the equally well-born Mewill. The spectacular activity of the last act, the explosion of coups de théâtre, is simply the fireworks celebrating the triumph of Kean's character.

Kean, like the *Portraits littéraires* of Sainte-Beuve, reflects the dominant romantic preoccupation with the man. But, as we have seen, Dumas would give us more than a superficial portrait; he would give voice to his portrait through the confessional of the play. Dramatic action, he retorts to Aristotle, *is* with a view to the representation of character; actions *do* come in as subsidiary to the character. And if in its portrait aspect *Kean* looks to Sainte-

Beuve, in its confessional aspect it looks to the so-called father of romanticism: "It's Rousseau's fault . . . ," writes a critic of romanticism, "Rousseau's and all his romantic disciples. In *Kean* did not Dumas go so far as to justify the excesses of the famous actor in assuring us that it was necessary to experience all the passions in order to be able to portray them on the stage?" [11]

With this criticism in mind, we can turn to the question of self-observation postponed earlier. When Salomon reproaches Kean for the life of debauch he is leading, Dumas's actor replies: "You are right, old friend, you are right. I feel that I am killing myself with this life of debauchery and orgies. But what would you have? I cannot change it. An actor must know all the passions in order to be able to express them well. I study them in myself; that's the way to know them by heart" (II.ii). Kean here seems to be subscribing to the subtlety observed in the theory of Villiers that "the actor experiences an emotion which is his own well enough, but which he lends to the character." [12] Though he remains within an esthetic of subjectivity by studying his own emotions, with the idea that he is in fact studying them, Kean moves toward a more objective conception. There is the suggestion that while he is presenting passions during a play, he is possibly not actually feeling them. Self-observation thus provides an alternative to Diderot's polarities. Though there is an identity of agent, there is a discrepancy of time. To the degree that this is true, however, Dumas's *Kean*, like Sartre's in a different connection, suffers from an error of conception. For it is Kean's own complaint that the bane of his profession is that one must go on to play Falstaff when one feels more like Hamlet, must go on to play Romeo when one feels like Falstaff.

For Kean is an actor without imagination. He is incapable of *dédoublement*. He does not "represent," unless we mean by that word neither "stand for" nor "imitate" but *"re*-present." The images which Kean's imagination conceives are only images of himself. Kean would not have to suffer Rousseau's general proscription of the actor: "Just what is the actor's talent? It is the art of the counterfeit, of dressing oneself up in another personality, of appearing different from what one is, of becoming impassioned in cold blood, of saying what one does not think as naturally as if one really thought it; finally, of forgetting one's own place in order to take someone else's." [13] Paradoxically enough, Rousseau's moralizing puts him on the same side, esthetically, as Diderot's first debater and Sartre's Kean: all three regard the actor as a liar, all three see a dissociation between actor and role. But this cannot apply to Dumas's Kean, who gives himself only for what he is "au théâtre comme à la taverne." (Dumas, I hasten to add, agrees more than he disagrees with Rousseau: the so-called father of romanticism indicts the play as a lie from the same compulsion which drives Dumas's actor to see it as a confessional—the need for sincerity.) Life takes the stage—Pirandello once again? Hardly, for in the Italian dramatist it is truly an action (in the Aristotelian sense) which is the subject of the play: human life, not *a* human life. Moreover, Pirandello's controlling conception is paradoxical: he attempts to demonstrate the superiority of life over art not in an essay or a tract but within a work of art. Dumas's *Kean* is basically antiparadoxical: there are not two orders, art and life or illusion and reality, but only one continuous order of undifferentiated experience.

This conception suggests the manner in which *Kean, Adrienne Lecouvreur,* or, for that matter, any play might be played: the actor has only to be himself. In the particular cases of *Kean* and *Adrienne* there seems to have been an especially felicitous mating of role and actor in the original presentations. "There," wrote a contemporary of Frédérick Lemaître in the role of Kean, "is all of Frédérick, one must say. In this play more than in any other, he was himself." [14] And the nostalgically romantic Gautier doubted that "Kean himself would have played his role better," [15] while a romantic from across the border, Heine, felt that ". . . there is a true creation, a real picture of England, and I believed I was seeing before my very eyes the late Edmund Kean, whom I have seen so many times." [16] As for the great Rachel in *Adrienne,* Legouvé tells a typical story. At a midnight rehearsal of the death scene, soon before the play was to open, Legouvé congratulated Rachel for the conviction with which she had rendered the scene. He attributed this to the fact that "there was no one there to applaud you and so you did not think about creating an effect, and you became in your own eyes poor Adrienne dying in the middle of night in the arms of two friends." But the actress cor-

rected him with: "You haven't understood at all! Something far
stranger happened to me, it was not over Adrienne that I was
crying, but myself. I don't know what told me that I would die
young like her; it seemed to me that I was in my own room, at
my final hour, that I was spectator at my own death scene. Thus
when, at the phrase, 'Farewell, triumphs of the theater, farewell,
excitements of an art I have loved so much,' you saw me shed true
tears, it was because I thought, with despair, that time would
carry off every trace of my talent and that soon there would
remain no more of her who had been Rachel." [17] Life, Legouvé
and Rachel would have us believe, invades the stage.

And yet, as we suggested earlier in the case of *Adrienne* (above,
p. 95), it is, ironically, the reverse which is true: the stage invades life, the person is lost in the impersonation. Paraphrasing
the philosopher George Mead, Lionel Trilling has referred to impersonation as a new mode of thought appropriate to that "new
sense of self" which is characteristically romantic. "Impersonation," Trilling recalls from Mead, "is the self's method of defining
itself." [18] This would mean, in the case of an actor, that the actor
expresses various facets of his personality through his various roles.
But we may justly wonder, in the case of *Kean,* if in place of the
spontaneous personality it is simply the preconceived personage
which comes through the role. This is strictly true, of course, in
the sense that neither *Kean* nor *Adrienne Lecouvreur* is factually
faithful to the lives of their subjects. It is also true, however, in
the sense that it is not even the actors (Rachel and Frédérick) or
the authors (Legouvé and Dumas) whose lives invade the stage.
For the lives which take the stage in *Kean* and *Adrienne,* whoever's lives they purport to be, are very unlifelike; they are book-
ish lives. The sense of self of all these artists is highly literary;
Kean and Adrienne are, so to speak, etymologically romantic:

> . . . *romantic* [writes a noted semanticist] is like *interesting,*
> *charming, exciting,* and many other adjectives, one of those
> modern words which describes not so much the objective
> qualities of things, as our response to them, the feelings they
> arouse in the susceptible spectator . . . if we examine the
> special subjective feeling described by *romantic,* we see that

it is a literary emotion (as indeed the derivation of the word from *romant* implies); it is Nature seen through the medium of literature, through a mist of associations derived from poetry and fiction.[19]

Or, derived, as in the case of our artists, from the stage. It is this same insight which, to the extent that the adaptation constitutes a critique, lies at the heart of Sartre's nihilistic *Kean*. The self which the romantic Kean confesses on the stage is a self born on the stage. Sartre finds the conception appalling. As for Dumas, does not his actor prove to Mewill and Eléna that the stage is the only realm of true value?

Chapter 8. Schnitzler and Pirandello

I. Schnitzler. The Play as Clinic

> POLONIUS: Give o'er the play.
> *Hamlet* (III.ii)

ALTHOUGH La Ronde, a recent movie version of Arthur Schnitzler's *Reigen* (*The Round Dance,* 1896–97), presented the dialogues of the faithless lovers as playlike episodes introduced by a carnival impresario standing before his carousel, the original presents them in an uncommented, clinically austere succession of exposures more in the nature of X-ray pictures than of playlets. Of course, the title and the form (the hypocrisy—or play-acting, as the Greek etymon of the word tells us—of the members of this human chain) do suggest some formalized play-acting taking place within a larger context, but the overeager French movie-maker has only been the victim of Schnitzler's irony by giving shape to the implied play within a play. The producer's "sophistication" has here been abetted by the star system of the movie industry: one feels that the impresario is presenting not The Young Wife but Danielle Darrieux playing The Young Wife; not The Count but Gérard Philipe playing The Count; etc. Yet in refusing to provide a frame, Schnitzler has seen what the movie-maker has not, that the play within a play is a double-edged device. With respect to the spectator's relationship to the outer play, the play within a play is an associative device ("how can people who are looking at a play be unreal?"); conversely, with respect to the spectator's relationship to the play within a play itself, the device is dissociative ("like me, those onstage spectators are looking at a play, something unreal"). Not surprisingly, then, the movie version of Schnitzler's corrosive commentary on modern sexual mores robs the original of much of its bite by providing a psychological cushion in the frame. If the spectator sees himself in any of the

characters in the movie version, it is only in the supercilious and
superficial impresario who transforms Schnitzler's caustic slices of
life into a bedroom farce. But by clearly implying yet deliberately
suppressing the frame, Schnitzler found the perfect formal expression of the message of his play: morality or convention is only
implied in human relationships; fidelity is honored more in the
breach than in the practice. Schnitzler, as Eric Bentley has observed, "starts from a frame and lets his characters walk out of it
into real life." [1]

If this relationship between illusion and reality was implicit in
Reigen, it became explicit and specifically theatrical in *Der Grüne
Kakadu* (*The Green Cockatoo,* 1899). Prosper, a former theater
manager, runs a Parisian cellar tavern, The Green Cockatoo,
where members of his old troupe entertain the nobility of the
tottering old regime by playing at rogues and criminals. There
is no scenario, no formal stage direction, no spatial division between actors and spectators; there are only customers and servers.
This occasionally leads to mistakes in timing: one actor, Scaevola,
for example, begins to play his role of bumptious drunkard a little
too soon, before there are any customers, in fact, so that Prosper
has to remind him to desist until there are some people to appreciate his antics. Even when the spectator-customers have arrived,
the actors, as far as one can tell, are merely themselves, talking
somewhat about themselves but mostly about the affairs of these
great days just before the fall of the Bastille. The tavern, in fact,
seems to be a sort of refuge from these harrowing events, and the
sense of its unreality and isolation from the bloody world outside
is underscored by the bizarre, mixture of illusion and reality of
the "entertainment." There is apparently no connection between
the great Revolution and the fanciful action within the tavern.

It is even difficult to speak of an "action" within the tavern, at
least in terms of a story having a beginning, a middle, and an end.
It seems better to speak of a number of false starts, interrupted
middles, and perplexing ends. Characters exist out of context, as
it were. There is Grain, otherwise known as Carniche or Shriek-
ing Pumice-Stone, an ex-criminal, who has murdered his aunt
and has now come to Prosper looking for a job. Prosper hires him
as an actor, but only on condition that he give himself for no more
than what he is: the murderer of his aunt. There are the street-

walkers, Flipotte and Michette, who sit in the laps of the young
aristocratic spectators, Albin and François. There has apparently
been some kind of an affair between Michette and Scaevola, the
actor-drunkard, for the latter becomes very jealous when Michette
plays up to young Albin. But this is taken back when the actor
apologizes to Prosper for having played this jealous bit too well.
Then there is Henri, the reigning actor and principal drawing
card of Prosper's bizarre theater. He wants to give up acting, for
he has just married Léocadie, also an actress and the reigning
whore of the environs, with whom he hopes to achieve a kind of
fairy-tale happiness in which her crowded past will cease to exist.
Henri's language and behavior, like those of his new wife, set
him off as a person of great importance in the play; yet our interest is once more abruptly diverted, this time to an equally bizarre
character, the Duke de Cadignan, whose wistful reflections on art
and life make him an exception among the frivolous aristocrats
who come to see Prosper's "plays." Finally, we meet the most
frivolous of these in the person of the Marquise Séverine de
Lansac, the patronizing and lascivious seductress of young men
who has come to Prosper's tavern only to make new conquests.

The action of the play is disparate and disjointed. It remains
out of focus for almost three-fourths of its duration, that is, until
the moody Henri returns upon the scene to announce that he has
killed his wife's last lover. His somber announcement coincides
with the news from the street that the Bastille has fallen and that
the Revolution is in full swing. The politically elated Prosper
tells Henri that he is glad to hear of the death of another noble-
man, the Duke de Cadignan, whom he had long known to be Léocadie's lover. This identification startles Henri, who has actually
only been playing his last and greatest bit for Prosper, but it also
has the effect of stimulating him to the real murder of the duke
when the latter bursts into the tavern amidst the hustle and bustle
of the revolutionary turmoil.

Now the murder of the duke seems anticlimactic and pointless.
He has been the most sympathetic of the royalists and if any of the
nobles was to be the victim, one would expect it to be the con-
temptuous, patronizing Séverine. Again, the real murder seems
the unreal one, so simple and swift is it compared to the elaborate,
imaginary murder Henri had described a few minutes earlier.

It seems pointless, too, that it should be Emile, from among all Léocadie's lovers, who should die at the hands of the jealous husband. Emile was not only the noblest in spirit of that amorous legion but he alone had a kind of Aristotelian awareness of Léocadie's virtue as a prostitute: "Could anything be more unreasonable than to take people away from their true calling? . . . I am not joking. Whores are born, not made—just as conquerors and poets are." [2] But Emile's death is not pointless; rather, it defines retrospectively the structure of *The Green Cockatoo:* that of the reversal or revolution. Henri is not only the jealous mate who slays his wife's lover; he is the actor-menial who slays the spectator-master.

Paralleling the political revolution taking place outside in the streets is an esthetic revolution taking place within the tavern. Schnitzler has repeated the dramaturgy of *The Round Dance* in *The Green Cockatoo,* but has added one convolution to his series. The frame or invisible play is the revolution taking place outside; the play within a play is all that we see going on in the tavern; the play within a play within a play is the "entertainment" which Prosper offers his customers (Scaevola's drunkenness, Henri's false murder, etc.). Thus Schnitzler has this time implied as an outer frame not the sentimental cushion of people playfully watching a merry-go-round or a round dance but the bloody events of an *actual* revolution. Furthermore, he has presented as a *visible* outer frame the make-believe of Prosper's tavern with the deliberate purpose, to recall Bentley, of "letting his characters walk out of it into real life." Under the old regime the theater, like Prosper's tavern, was not a part of real life. It was a storehouse of emotional curios, a rummage shop for the idle aristocracy, which came never to buy (that is, to be truly affected), but only to browse. The ultimately indifferent spectators came to see only the fake passions of a Scaevola for a Michette or of a Henri for a Léocadie, only false pickpockets like Etienne and Maurice. But on this occasion, the spectators are the victims of their own intentions: having come to see the unreal, when they do see true passion and real thievery before their eyes, they insist upon taking them for fakes. Yet the crimes they witness are real acts, not mere acting. The actors inside the tavern, like the masses outside, overthrow their old masters, the spectator-nobles, in order to show their emancipation from old conventions and old laws.

Schnitzler merges the twin revolutions in the twin murders committed by Henri at the end of the play: the false one of his wife's legendary last lover and the real murder of his wife's real last lover, the duke. But it would be misleading to regard *The Green Cockatoo* on the one hand, as a political parable with esthetic overtones, or on the other as an esthetic manifesto with political overtones. Neither political philosopher nor esthetician, Schnitzler has told us the story of the revolutionary actors as a psychological tale with moral overtones. Henri's transformation from would-be assassin into real assassin expresses once again the central theme of so many of Schnitzler's plays: the birth of awareness, the deliberate disillusioning of self, the courageous confrontation of reality for what it is. The dramatist never completely confuses us as to what is real and what unreal in the plot of his play. The apparent interchangeability of the two planes of action in *The Green Cockatoo* is really a piece of sleight-of-hand, achieved chiefly by the suppression of a theatrical setting for his inner play. We soon catch on to the fact that the actors are not acting. Prosper's name consciously evokes that of Prospero, Shakespeare's magician-artist who also created his effects for real. When the literal-minded revolutionary philosopher Grasset demands direct revolutionary action, berating the theater as a futile instrument of social change, Prosper reminds him that in the theater he can "insult . . . to my heart's content — while they take it for a joke" and that "one fine day there will come along the time when the jest turns to earnest." And other developments advise us that the actors of *The Green Cockatoo* are not acting, that they are putting illusion behind them. For example, Schnitzler sets up a kind of algebraic problem in our minds, but one whose solution he wishes us to see immediately, when he shows us the murderer Grain being hired to play himself as a murderer. If, we say to ourselves, the real criminal is to become an actor, no doubt the actor-criminals will become criminals: which is, of course, what happens.

We are, then, left with no doubts about the relationship between the real and the unreal. They are reversed from Marivaux, with the reversal being unreal into real. We do not have the mingling of the real and the unreal, their perplexing fusion as in

Pirandello and much twentieth-century drama. Only the surface
of Schnitzler is "soft" and what we have come to think of as
"Chekhovian" (just as perhaps only the surface of Chekhov himself is Chekhovian). The inner structure of *The Green Cockatoo*
is hard and tough, as hard and as tough as the French Revolution.
The dramaturgy never really moves off center: two of the apparently most pointless characters, Albin and François, the aristocratic spectators, actually keep the play in constant focus for the
attentive spectator and, more importantly, define the latter's relationship to the theme of courageous consciousness which the
play develops. Albin and François are the only characters to be
present on the stage throughout almost the entire play; like the
spectators of *The Green Cockatoo,* they do not move from their
seats. They are, in fact, the surrogates of the spectators of Schnitzler's play. Between them they epitomize the two principles upon
which the idea of a theater depends: dissociation and identification. Albin is constantly taken in by what he sees, while François
constantly dismisses his companion's fears as alarmist and naive.
That it is Albin, the spectator who identifies with the "actors,"
whom events prove right measures for us the distance we have
traveled from Marivaux. All was not in jest; the game has been
played for keeps.

   Through Albin is Schnitzler paradoxically preaching the renunciation of the theater? Certainly, what Bentley has called the
"refined realism" [3] of his technique would find in such a thesis
a consistent philosophical extension. True to its premises, naturalism denies the duality of the theater: suppressing the principle
of dissociation, it gives free rein to that of identification. Familiar
naturalistic formulas betray this bias: "slice of life," "thesis play,"
"documentary approach," etc. One senses a negative filiation with
the romantic conception of the theater in the suppression of the
principle of dissociation. Beyond this, however, the conceptions
differ: where romantic identification was based on a view of reality
as becoming and transformation, naturalistic identification is
based on a view of reality as being and continuation. Now very
likely this peculiar esthetic problem and its attendant paradoxes
did not as such interest Schnitzler. At best, if he felt some logic had
to be appealed to in the face of his implicit *"anti-*esthetic," good
doctor that he was he could have evoked the analogy of the im-

munization from a disease which results from a small dosage of the disease. But there is no need to force such doctrinal consistencies upon him, because, like all true artists, he cannot be wholly caught within the narrow confines of a doctrinaire movement. More specifically, the subject of *The Green Cockatoo* is not really the idea of the theater—naturalistic or otherwise. (In fact, around this time, with Hofmannsthal and others, Schnitzler formed "Young Vienna," an antinaturalist group.) Schnitzler is really concerned here in this early work with the problem of personality. He is a clinical psychologist sensitively but dispassionately listening to a patient tell of his problems.

The dramatist has properly found the "objective correlative" of this clinical situation. The form of *The Green Cockatoo* is not that of the unilinear "documentary" one might expect from the ostensible subject matter (the French Revolution). Indeed, with its abrupt shifts of interest in a rapid series of scenes, the dramaturgy of *The Green Cockatoo* moves away from the literal-mindedness of the typical naturalistic play as document toward the more freewheeling "naturalism" of the film. Here I would like to apply to the structure of this play some remarks which Susanne K. Langer has applied more generally to the film:

> Cinema is "like" dream in the mode of its presentation: it creates a virtual present, an order of direct apparition. That is the mode of dream.
>
> The most noteworthy formal characteristic of dream is that the dreamer is always at the center of it. Places shift, persons act and speak or change or fade—facts emerge, situations grow, objects come into view with strange importance, ordinary things infinitely valuable or horrible, and they may be superseded by others that are related to them essentially by feeling, not by natural proximity. But the dreamer is always "there," his relation is, so to speak, equidistant from all events.[4]

The filmlike surface of Schnitzler's play is that of dream and the dreamer is Schnitzler's spectator who witnesses the shifting events of the dream through his half-participating, half-dissociated surrogate, Albin-François. If the clear-eyed dramatist invites us to identify not with François who refuses to take the lessons of his dream seriously but with Albin, it is not merely to indulge himself in the paradoxes of an antiesthetic esthetic. Rather, to the dramatist's attentive psychologist, Albin plays the good patient who sees that those who dream in his dream, the actors of Prosper's "play," put their illusions behind them and, "being awak'd, do despise the dream" (*Henry IV*, Pt. I. Act v). Disillusion in Schnitzler means not disappointment but discovery.

II. Pirandello. The Play as Life

> . . . this is an art
> Which does mend nature, change it rather, but
> The art itself is nature.
>
> *The Winter's Tale* (IV.iv)

For all his interest in personality, Schnitzler is still very far from the romantic cult of the ego. The loose, episodic structure of the *Round Dance* and of *The Green Cockatoo* is not designed to dramatize the qualities or defects of any single character; rather, Schnitzler uses it to point to the variety and extent of personality disorders in the modern world. Not a personality but personality *in function* is the subject of such plays. Thus both spiritually and chronologically he stands on the threshold of twentieth-century drama, which, in one of its major phases, returns to the classical, Aristotelian conception of the drama as the study not of a man but of an action. The drama, to paraphrase Luigi Pirandello, one of the leading exponents of this renewed conception, ceases to be historical (i.e., biographical) and becomes philosophical.[5]

Twenty years ago Pirandello, like Freud, was more talked about than read. Though neither of these great seminal minds has to this day totally escaped this fate, modern criticism does feel that it has achieved some understanding of them based on a careful analysis of their works. Unfortunately, it has done so only at the expense of considerable revision of certain essential notions. In an earlier phase, just as Freud criticism practically substituted the adjective "Freudian" for the much used "sexual," so Pirandello criticism substituted "Pirandellian" for such familiar words as "illusory" and "intellectual." Most of this "criticism" became exasperated with Pirandello's elaborate intellectual conceits, dismissing them as a kind of *marivaudage* in the tragic mode; it seldom devoted itself to a real effort to resolve the master's en-meshed paradoxes. Nowadays, in fact, Pirandellian revisionists caution us against such sterile pursuits. They tell us to give greater heed to the adjective in the over-all title which Pirandello gave to his theater: *Naked Masks.* "Pirandellian" is fast coming to mean "passionate," that is, etymologically, "suffering." We must no longer try to *understand* Pirandello; we must *feel* him. Such a view of this thinking playwright only reflects, of course, the modern retreat from reason. It represents another ripple on the wave of anti-intellectualism which has engulfed the western world since the First World War in manifestations as sophisti-cated as the cult of D. H. Lawrence and as coarse as McCarthyism. I do not mean to underestimate Pirandello's own share in this attack upon reason nor would I, in a paradox to undo all Piran-dellian paradoxes, draw a portrait of him as a Cartesian rationalist in Freudian sheep's clothing. But, fully acknowledging the depth and significance of passion in his theater, I believe it is time to call a halt to the deintellectualization of Pirandello's theater of ideas—time, once again, to understand Pirandello.

The typical Pirandellian structure is the reversed reversal. We are shown one view of a situation, which is then reversed by the introduction not of a new event but simply of a new viewer (or of the old viewer suddenly switching sides); however, this reversal is in turn reversed by the introduction of still another viewer. The movement is circular: we wind up where we began with the uneasy feeling that we are about to begin all over again. For ex-ample, in the 1917 play *Così è (se vi pare),* probably the best known of the plays outside of *Sei personaggi in cerca d'autore,* we are first led to believe in Signor Ponza's version of his own rela-tions with the woman he calls his second wife, rather than the version of Signora Frola: the woman is his second wife whom he shields from his "mad" mother-in-law in order to spare her the painful discovery that the woman is not her daughter, his long-dead first wife. But Ponza leaves the scene only to have Signora Frola return with the equally believable tale that she only pre-tends to be mad in order to let Ponza cherish his illusion of a second marriage, but the unseen woman *is* her daughter, his first wife, who has returned to him after a stay in a mental institution.

Now, this pattern is quickly recognized as that of the comedy of errors, as ancient as Menander and Terence and Plautus, as familiar as Shakespeare and Molière and Marivaux. But Pirandello has added a new twist: in him there is no external, fixed reality to which one can cling in the constant shifting of the action, in him no social code of good faith to which all can appeal as the ultimate sincerity. Not Philinte, Molière's *honnête homme* and champion of *bon sens,* but Laudisi, the jeering relativist and confusing spinner of paradoxes, is Pirandello's *raisonneur.* "It is so (if you think so)"—"each in his own way"—"dream, but perhaps not"—the Pirandellian world is a market place of what children call "Indian-giving": give only to take back. Truth is relative; it is what *you* and *you* and *you* make of it. There are as many truths about any situation as there are viewers of that situation. And the objection of "logical contradictions" is meaningless: one man's truth is as good as another's, for each man can see only his own truth.

The structural implication of such a conception is obvious: there can be no solution to the problem of the play, or, in the familiar language of drama criticism, there can be no resolution of the conflict. Yet we cannot deny that we do sense some resolution in Pirandello—almost, as it were, in spite of his bewildering superstructure of paradoxes. For there are in Pirandello's dramaturgy two conflicts: the ostensible and the real. The ostensible conflict occurs between those whom Eric Bentley has described as the "busybodies" on the one side, and, on the other, those "sufferers" whose suffering is only aggravated by the nosy probings of the others.[6] Typically, this conflict between the Agazzis and the Ponzas-Frolas (the sides in *Così è*) remains unresolved because, as Francis Fergusson has put it, Pirandello "accepts his paradoxes as various versions of a final split in human nature and destiny itself."[7] But underlying the ostensible conflict, which really exists as a kind of play within a play, is the real one: between the sufferers themselves, between the Ponzas and the Frolas. Pirandello resolves this conflict in a number of ways, all usually involving to some degree a contrapuntal use of the ostensible conflict. In *Così è* the consonance of opinion between the Ponzas and the Frolas clashes with the dissonance of opinion among the Agazzis and their neighbors. The dissonance is always attempting to break through in order to reduce the consonance to *the dissonance it also once was.* For the accord between the Ponzas and the Frolas represents the resolution of a prior conflict, one which is in constant danger of recurring. Like so many other of Pirandello's plays, *Così è* reverses normal dramatic development: it moves from resolution through exposition. "There is a misfortune here," the woman in black says at the end of the play, ". . . which must stay hidden: otherwise the remedy which our compassion has found cannot avail" (Act III). The remedy *has been found*—and found even before the play begins. The real conflict is preresolved, but Pirandello achieves dramatic tension in the threat of dissolution represented by the relentless inquiries of the busybodies.

Thus illusion triumphs, but not, as in Molière, because it is the sign of life's possibilities, the key notion of a comic view of life, but only because it makes life bearable: it is the remedy which compassion finds for life's ills. In Molière, we remember, it was "the others" who held a firm grip on reality, who, in playing their little plays, were only accommodating themselves to the fantasy of the ridiculous figure. In Pirandello, relationships are exactly reversed: it is the isolated characters (the Ponzas-Frolas) who accommodate themselves to some irreducible fact, while the others or busybodies insist on a one-dimensional approach to reality. Hence, since the stubborn fact involved is the tragic limitation of the human condition, while the mechanism of adjustment to it is comic accommodation rather than tragic acceptance, we may describe Pirandello as a "comitragedian," applying to most of his plays that phrase which Gide so wrongheadedly applied to Molière's *Le Malade imaginaire:* "une farce tragique."

Are we, then, to except from this designation the trilogy of plays—*Sei personaggi in cerca d'autore* (1921), *Ciascuno a suo modo* (1924), and *Questa sera si recita a soggetto?* (1930)—which constitutes Pirandello's theater about the theater? Perhaps out of a compulsion for sincerity which we might expect in such intensely self-conscious writing, Pirandello seems to abandon the peculiar mixture of comic form and tragic outlook. The comic form (that is, the mechanism of accommodation) is deliberately and overtly disallowed: the busybodies are invited to leave the scene (*Sei personaggi*), frustrated in their efforts to manipulate things to their own satisfaction (*Ciascuno a suo modo*), literally chased from the scene by the "sufferers" (*Questa sera*). In these plays the sufferers no longer wish to make some accommodation to reality in order to make it bearable; rather, in various degrees they live their suffering before our very eyes. This time, the busybodies—that is, the actors and directors—would make some kind of accommodation, here in the form of the necessary restrictions which art imposes upon life. And since here, as usual, the busybodies are the unsympathetic characters of the plays, it is as if the master were turning his back upon the solutions he himself has always proposed. Now he bares the suffering rather than merely hinting at it. More, since it is the people of the theater who are chased in the name of life, it seems as if the dramatist were denying his own art. Passion and compassion are allowed to run their course; life, as Francis Fergusson puts it, takes the stage.

It does so, however, to a greater degree in some plays than in others. Indeed, the three plays of the theater about the theater show in chronological order Pirandello's increasing success as he attempted to find that form which would perfectly objectify his particular understanding of the theater and of all art as a "naked mask."

That the "six characters" do not find their author points at once to the success and the limitations as a work of art of the play in which they have found an author, *Sei personaggi*. For they are really looking not for an author but for a play. We remember that they have already been created in a "certain author's" mind when they come upon the stage, so that what they are really seeking is another author to finish their story in that total form we call a play. Thus Pirandello seems to have conceived *Sei personaggi* in order to prove *negatively* Aristotle's conception of tragedy as an action. But at the same time he is pointing to his own affirmation of the greater truth of artistic reality over living reality, for the six characters, fictions within a fiction, are undeniably more real to us in their sufferings than the shallow members of the acting company. The very subject of the present play (the necessity for character to have its story dramatized in the totality of a work of art) prevents Pirandello from showing us these characters in a truly tragic action: *Sei personaggi* is condemned by its own terms to be almost totally ostensible plot, that is, the highly abstract quarrel between the troupe on the one hand

and the characters on the other. The real plot, the conflict between the members of the family (particularly between the stepdaughter and the father), is, again by the very terms of the play, prevented from achieving resolution. Such a resolution could occur only in some imaginary play within a play, and Pirandello, as we know, cannot give us that play here without voiding his present purposes.

As J.-Th. Paolanonacci has observed, the mode of *Sei personaggi* is narrative rather than dramatic.[8] Various members of the family (principally the father) tell the story of the family, and all this, as both the father and the stage director realize, is undramatic, a mere prologue. The older boy apart, each of the six characters really relives only two moments of the story: first the crucial moment of suffering (the scene in Madame Pace's house of assignation where the father is about to take the stepdaughter but is stopped by the long-suffering mother in an eternal moment of shame for all three), and the final scene of the death of the two young children, with only the boy's suicide actually coming to us with some directness (we hear the shot and see the mother's pathetic reaction). The scene at Madame Pace's is, of course, the great moment of the play, but it is still only a moment of art, not a work of art. Pirandello's analogy (in his preface to the play) between the eternalized moment of suffering of the six characters and the eternalized embrace of Dante's Paolo and Francesca begs the question: the embrace of those immortal lovers is but one moment of many in a fully realized action; the embrace of Pirandello's lovers is the only moment of an otherwise unrealized action. In this, his first dramatized eulogy to eternal form, Pirandello has fixed for all time not life, nor even a slice of life, but one of life's gestures. Although the play does show us the members of the acting troupe preparing to put on the six characters' play (even getting so far as to play the travesty of the scene in Madame Pace's), the play never really does get put on. It is, to follow Pirandello's subtitle, only a play in the making. *Sei personaggi* being, then, almost all ostensible plot or outer play, the mechanism of dissociation functions almost exclusively. When the mechanism of identification does function briefly during the harrowing assignation scene, it leaves us only frustrated, feeling cheated when we do not get beyond this moment. Knowing that it could not be otherwise because Pirandello never intended to dramatize fully the family's conflict does not relieve our frustration.

But in *Ciascuno a suo modo,* which the dramatist described as a conflict between "The Spectators and the Author and the Actors," the real plot is dramatized rather than talked about. Indeed, it is more accurate to say that both real plots are dramatized, since Pirandello has doubled his action by truly giving us a play within a play—which is to say a Pirandellian play within a Pirandellian play, so we should not be astonished if the inner play is as involuted as the outer play. The ostensible plot of the inner play (which occupies the greater part of the running time of *Ciascuno*) involves the efforts of the busybodies to discover exactly what feelings prompted the notorious woman of the world, Delia Morello, to run off with her fiancé's brother-in-law on the eve of her marriage: was it to spare her fiancé the life of shame their marriage would have meant to him or was it sheer cruelty, just another of her infamous escapades? Delia herself seems hardly to understand her own motives, for she sides now with one of her champions, now with the other; and the champions of Delia do not know either which view to take, for each changes sides, so persuaded of his opponent's original position that he is ready to fight a duel with whoever defends his own original position. Mixing things up still further are the bewildering comments of the Laudisi of this play, Diego Cinci, who defends all views of Delia's actions. Meanwhile, behind all of this lies the real conflict between Delia and Michel Rocca, the brother-in-law with whom she ran off. The resolution occurs as Michel and Delia encounter one another at the home of Francesco Savio, one of Delia's busybody defenders.

The outer play repeats the relationship between the ostensible and the real plot. Here the ostensible conflict is the familiar literary one between the partisans and the enemies of Pirandello as they argue about whether anybody can really know just what Pirandello means. But, while the various busybodies argue in the abstract (although with considerable fervor) about what life means, the real conflict of life goes on pulsating about them: the conflict between those people whose real story has served as the basis of the *pièce à clef* which we have seen centering about Delia Morello. While everybody argues about whether Pirandello has the right to transcribe so literally upon the stage these real events so recently the subject of a public scandal, the real-life models for this study suddenly confront one another in the theater lobby and hurl themselves into each others' arms in spite of themselves —just like the lovers in the final scene of the play. Pirandello proves Wilde's epigram dramatically: "Nature imitates art." But in doing so, he resolves only the specifically artistic conflict of the play, that is, the ostensible conflict between the partisans of Pirandello and the enemies of Pirandello. Obviously Pirandello and his partisans have been proved right by this irrefutable evidence from life: the dramatist had every right to use this real event for it is only in doing so that he can remain true to his task as an artist. But this much having been proved, we are still left high and dry about the outcome of the destructive love between Delia Moreno and Baron Nutti—or, what comes to the same thing, between Delia Morello and Michel Rocca.

Nevertheless, the relationship between ostensible and real plot is dramatically more satisfying here than in *Sei personaggi*. Because when we first meet her we do not know that Delia Morello is only a character in a play, we identify with her (through either love or hate, but still becoming emotionally involved with her). *Ciascuno* begins with the inner play; the two planes of action merge and it is only after the first act, in the lobby scene, that we realize that this has all been a doubly unreal business. But in giving this knowledge to us at this point, Pirandello cuts off, as it were, the satisfaction we had felt in our identification with Delia Morello throughout the first act. Of course, when we return to the second act of what we now know to be the play within a play, Pirandello does continue to engage our sympathies in a way that the essentially narrative mode of *Sei personaggi* precluded; by dramatizing Delia Morello's own doubts about the reasons for her flighty affair with Michel Rocca, by presenting Delia and Michel as characters in a drama whose outcome they themselves do not know, Pirandello allows the mechanism of identification to function to a greater degree than in *Sei personaggi*. Nevertheless, once the interlude has defined Delia Morello's story as part of a play, we cannot help but feel about her and her fellow sufferers the way we felt about the six characters. That is, neither the six characters nor Delia can really overcome the strong barrier of dissociation which our knowledge of their double fictionality throws up. And this is just as Pirandello would have it, for he would have us identify not with Delia Morello but with Delia Moreno, the model from which he fashioned his Delia Morello.

Surprise (an appeal to the emotions) has replaced curiosity (an appeal to the intellect). Yet as dramatically satisfying as this is, it is not completely so. Though we are clearly involved in an action instead of just one moment of it (*Sei personaggi*), Pirandello still holds back: on the threshold of resolution, he stops his play. Delia Moreno and Baron Nutti leave us guessing about the outcome of their passion in exactly the same way as their fictional counterparts, Delia Morello and Michel Rocca. Dramatically speaking, we have exposition, crisis, but no denouement. *Ciascuno* is a play literally unmade, never completed, a tragedy without epiphany, a drama never resolved.

The play in the making but never made (*Sei personaggi*); the play unmade, begun, but never completed (*Ciascuno a suo modo*) —there remained only one formula for Pirandello in his trilogy of the theater about the theater: the play begun and completed, the play fully made. He called it *Questa sera si recita a soggetto.* In this final play about the theater, Pirandello returns to the formula of *Sei personaggi:* right from the outset we know we are in a fictional theater, the first persons we meet being various spectators and Doctor Hinkfuss, a stage director who presents himself as just that and no more. The variation of the formula comes in the actors. This time, it is they who see themselves in the way the six characters had earlier: the actors *are* the characters they play. "I simply want you to understand," The Leading Man tells Hinkfuss, "that, in these clothes, Mr. . . . [giving his own name] no longer exists; seeing that I have contracted with you to improvise tonight, by speaking whatever words may spring— spring!—from the part I play, accompanied by spontaneous action and with every gesture in place; Mr. . . . . [his own name] must *live* the part of *Rico Verri,* he must *be* Rico Verri." And, indeed, it is because he refuses to let the characters be themselves, because he constantly wishes to restore them to puppets, that Doctor Hinkfuss finally drives his actors to rebellion. In *Questa sera,* the ostensible plot and the real plot clash just as in *Sei personaggi,* but this time the busybodies (Hinkfuss and his assistants) are chased from the stage to allow the real plot to run its natural course. This course is the fully realized drama of a marriage destroyed by retrospective jealousy. Pirandello thus finds his way out of the structural impasse which left *Sei personaggi* unresolved and which he chose to resolve only partially in *Ciascuno a suo modo:* the resolution of both the ostensible and the real plots. By wresting the stage away from their director, the characters of *Questa sera,* bolder than their counterparts in *Sei personaggi,* resolve the ostensible plot and thus enable the real plot to achieve resolution.

Yet, when that resolution has been reached in the death of Mommina Verri, Doctor Hinkfuss suddenly rushes forward from the rear of the theater, shouting words of approval to the actors for the way they have played out the drama. For he did not leave the theater, after all; instead he slipped out of view in order to direct the technicians in the use of the lights and props. For the director can never be chased—though foolish ones can be admonished. Hinkfuss' reappearance reminds us that Rico Verri and Mommina are *personaggi* and that theirs has been a play within a play, that the director himself has been an actor. Ostensible plot and real plot merge, for life (the real plot) can find enduring form only in art (the ostensible plot). Hinkfuss' reappearance only makes explicit what the pyrotechnics of the earlier theater plays blinded us from seeing: that Pirandello has been singing the superiority of life over form within the form of art. Hinkfuss teaches us that, ultimately, we cannot except Pirandello's trilogy of the theater about the theater from the morality we have derived from his other plays: illusion, or form, or ostensible plot is an indispensable part of the human condition. We must argue about the meaning of the passions which life thrusts upon us, we must try to give some form to them, we must live according to some convention or illusion in order to make life bearable. "This is the remedy which compassion finds." To be sure, life will undo the forms we impose upon it—the most telling of all Pirandello's paradoxes is that death is really an excess of life, a cancerous growth which spends the body in which it exists—and Pirandello's plays do record this defeat. But there is no reason to despair, for they record as well the victory born of that defeat: if it is man's fate to lose the struggle with life everywhere else, in one sphere he may win that struggle—in that living illusion, the only form which endures: the work of art. "All that lives," Pirandello has written, "by the fact of living, has a form, and by the same token must die—except the work of art which lives forever in so far as it *is* form." [9] Mommina's tragedy—the "life which took the stage" —reaches the tragic epiphany, we recall, within a work of art: as she sings from *Il Trovatore*.

Art denuded is still art. *Sei personaggi, Ciascuno a suo modo, Questa sera* may strip human passions to their *naked* reality, but we see this nakedness only in the *mask* of Pirandello's art. Like Molière, Pirandello invites us to the view of human life as itself theatrical. However, the mask which the modern Italian sees as an integral part of reality is not the smiling visage of comedy, but the downcast countenance of tragedy. What makes one man a comedian and the other a tragedian is more the affair of the psychologist than the drama critic. Suffice to say that Pirandello believes that the form which human life takes is tragic and that it is the duty of the artist to reflect that form in his art. Thus Pirandello's directors and actors are hooted from the stage not because they wish to impose a mask upon the seething passion of life, but because they wish to impose another mask upon one already there.

The actor, according to such a view, is false just when he is trying too hard to be himself by "editing" the role to his own personality; if he would only *be* the character, melt into *its* personality, the question of his own integrity as a person would then become irrelevant. In being true to his art the actor will be true perhaps to himself, but, more importantly, to life. This conception of the actor's art is obviously very different from romantic egocentricity. And, to the extent that Pirandello is uninterested in the chameleon-like capacities of the actor, it differs in emphasis, too, from Diderot's theory of the unfeeling actor. The actor's talents have nothing to do with it, as Pirandello sees it. He expresses a role, not *his* art. Pirandello's fascination with actors is a fascination with life itself, for is not the actor the ideal creature to depict that truth about every human being which Montaigne uttered nearly four centuries ago?: No man is so different from another than he is from himself at various stages of life. The actor, according to Pirandello, is called upon to dramatize not a life, but life itself. Not since Flaubert have we had an artist so wrongly accused of using his art as a personal confessional, for not since Flaubert have we had an artist so passionately concerned with the objectivity of the work of art. Art brings to Pirandello as to Flaubert that rare emotion which James Joyce associated almost exclusively with the creative act: joy.[10] Art is Pirandello's victory over life.

Chapter 9. Anouilh. The Play as Maze

> This is as strange a maze as e'er men trod;
> And there is in this business more than nature
> Was ever conduct of.
>
> *The Tempest* (v.i)

PIRANDELLO'S tragic mask replies to Molière's comic mask. It is a common belief that one must choose between the two as between God and Mammon. One view of life inevitably involves a reserving judgment of the other. Professional "tragic viewers" invariably look upon the comic view as shortsighted, naive, shallow, unrealistic. Professional "comic viewers" see the tragic view as equally shortsighted and, in its extreme phases, as dismal, death-centered, antihuman. Criticism has traditionally consigned writers to one or the other camp and seldom has it found itself embarrassed about locating any writer. Jean Anouilh represents one of those rare instances, for now he reflects in his *pièces noires* that somber, tragic view of life which is the mark of this "age of Pirandello," now he turns around and reflects in his *pièces roses* the comic view.

Nowhere has he more acutely expressed this rare double vision than in his theater about the theater. In fact, with the unimportant exception of Sacha Guitry, no modern French playwright has been more preoccupied with the theme of the theater than Anouilh. There is hardly a major Anouilh character, from the Lady Hurf of the early *Le Bal des voleurs* (written 1932) to the general of the more recent *La Valse des toréadors* (1952), who does not feel himself, whether willingly or not, to be the actor of a comédie. Lady Hurf thinks of herself as "an old woman covered with diamonds who plays at intrigues" and the general asks of his ex-actress wife: "What new play are you putting on now?" Indeed, *La Valse*, without containing a play within a play, offers us that conception of life as a play which we shall explore in a moment through Anouilh's use of that device. When the dejected general asks the doctor how the complicated farce they are in is going to end, the latter replies: "As in life—or as in the theater when it was still good: a prearranged ending, not too sad in appearance, of which no one is really the dupe—and, a little afterwards, curtain!" (v) Such, in fact, is the conclusion of *La Valse*, as the general discovers that Gaston, his secretary and rival for his mistress' favor, is his son. In the still more recent *L'Alouette* (1953), his retelling of Joan of Arc's story, Anouilh relies on a variant of the inner play, the flash back. The action begins late in Joan's story, with the heroine about to be judged, but through a series of flash backs we are enabled to see almost all of Joan's story before her burning at the stake: as she or her judges evoke the major moments of her previous life, the various personages involved come forth to "play" those moments. Indeed, thanks to this technique of the playlike flash back (the judges comment on the "acting" of the various personages), Anouilh is enabled to end his play not on the somber note of Joan's burning but on the joyous one of the most triumphant moment of her career: the crowning of the dauphin at Reims. As the firewood is heaped up about the bound Joan, Beaudricourt, one of her captains, rushes forth to halt the action, protesting: "We can't end it like that, my lord. We haven't played the coronation scene. We had been told that everything would be played. Joan has a right to the coronation, it's in her story!" *L'Alouette* is but one of the numerous echoes from the dramatic literature of the past which resound through Anouilh's repertory: *Eurydice, Antigone, Roméo et Jeannette, Médée*, etc. The repertory is acted out by his actors, ex-actors, and would-be actors to the accompaniment of music and in the figures of the dance (*La Valse, Le Bal, La Polka*). It is not surprising, then, that Anouilh has used the formula of the play within a play, or an approximation of it, over and over in his theater of some twenty-odd titles. The formula provides the ideal occasion for the dramatist to conduct his theatrically centered investigation of the theme of appearance and reality. Indeed, it is through this technique, raised to the level of a structural metaphor of the most telling force in *Colombe*, that he is enabled to project his special vision of life as a mixture of *rose* and *noir*, now a tragicomedy, now a comitragedy.

In *Le Bal des voleurs* a group of professional thieves, pretending to be noblemen in order to gain access to the jewels of one
Lady Hurf, find themselves thieves in spite of themselves. For
they are asked to play at thieves in Lady Hurf's impromptu "bal
des voleurs," which she has created primarily in order to relieve
her boredom. In this bal des voleurs which she has created out of
the officially announced "bal des fleurs" (telling only her ward
Eva of the change), she reminds us of Marivaux's Mme Amelin:
the play is primarily a game. But the real informs the illusory:
her ward, Juliette, falls in love with one of the thieves playing at
being thieves and runs off with him. Lady Hurf had accepted as
part of her game that the believable make-believe thieves would
make off with her jewelry, but not with her niece. However, she
is a good sport who accepts the further price. Besides, is she not
indemnified when the police seize those fakers whose real thievery
becomes visible only in the bal des voleurs? For the Dupont-
Dufort, father and son, are the true thieves in *Le Bal des voleurs*,
and when the police seize them in their thieves' get-up and carry
them off to jail, it is more than poetic justice: putting on the
theatrical thieves' robes, the father and son had only turned themselves inside out to show their true natures. The affection they
show the women is false; they love Lady Hurf and her wards only
for their money. But the professional thieves? Why, they have
been sincere in Lady Hurf's play: they have only been themselves. Reality triumphs not over but in illusion. The unauthentic
is the image of the authentic.

Though listed as a pièce rose, *Le Rendez-vous de Senlis* (1937)
is more accurately described as a pièce noire which becomes a
pièce rose, thus reversing the relationship (somewhat muted) in
Le Bal. Georges, a young man who has been ruthlessly married off
by his ambitious family to a rich girl he does not love, tries to find
happiness by constructing an illusory set of relationships between
himself and an ideal mother, father, and best friend. At an intimate dinner party he plans for the ideal yet unexpectedly actual
mistress he has finally found, the mother and father are to be
played by professional actors. Georges's greatest difficulty with
the latter is to make them give up their conventional stage conceptions of the roles they are to play. Like Lady Hurf, Georges
is hoping to find reality in his illusion, but, as contrasted with

Lady Hurf, he is hoping to make his players not actors in spite of themselves but people in spite of themselves. So Georges has prepared the stage of his castle-theater and all that is awaited is the series of blows signalizing the start of the play, the knock of his mistress upon the door. But when Georges is called away by a mysterious message in the most theatrical fashion, his actors tell all to Isabelle even before the play gets started. Isabelle, however, instead of being offended with Georges is offended with the treacherous actors, treacherous because they have refused to play out their deceit for her. And when Georges returns to his disenchanted castle, it is Isabelle who, simply by being herself, enables him to live briefly—five minutes—but happily in his play world. As with Juliette's love in Lady Hurf's comedy, the love of Georges and Isabelle, the only truth "in the midst of so many lies," enables him to find reality in illusion.

Yet the five minutes are enough to make Georges, recovered from a gunshot wound he has received from his wife, see that the real comedy was going on not at the "rendez-vous de Senlis" but in the sad reality he had tried to forget through his play: the "comedy" in which his greedy parents drove him into a loveless marriage, and in which he treated his best friend as a lackey and his friend's wife as a *fille de joie*. Georges gives up this pièce noire in order to play in the pièce rose he has created with Isabelle. When the actors of the pièce noire have left, Georges sits down to his play table in order to dine with his "real" mother and father and with his real mistress; Isabelle and the hired actors. But it is perhaps the presence of the actors which makes the discovery of reality in illusion, though carried beyond that of *Le Bal*, seem as unstable here as in the earlier play. The illusion with its attendant reality does not promise to be an enduring one: not only will the lease on the castle run out in one month and the actors return to their real theaters, but the castle itself is, after all, only a fake theater. For a more enduring representation of the triumph of reality in illusion we shall have to wait for *Colombe*.

In *Léocadia* (written 1939), as in *Le Rendez-vous*, the heroine, the sincere Amanda, is likewise invited to play a role in the hero's play: literally a replaying of the past as young Albert relives his adventure with the playful Léocadia, his mistress whose death has left him forlorn. Struck by Amanda's remarkable resemblance to the dead *chanteuse,* Albert's aunt, the duchess, has wanted to bring the latter back in the measure that such a thing is possible through an impersonation, just as she has brought back—quite literally—to her estate the scenes of Albert's and Léocadia's affair. At first Amanda refuses, but upon seeing Albert for the first time, she agrees.

Now when this first encounter occurs, Amanda, at the behest of the duchess, has grudgingly agreed to repeat Léocadia's purported first words to Albert. But the young man answers the rehearsed question about the way to the sea quite automatically, as if it were asked in good faith. He takes Amanda for Amanda, or, since he does not know her, at least not for Léocadia. We soon learn why, when he explains his reason for agreeing to play in his aunt's play. He does so not because he has remembered the past so well but because he has so much difficulty in remembering it. The difference is crucial: for his forgetfulness in spite of his at- tachment to Léocadia reveals a greater readiness to live in the present than Albert is willing to admit. Amanda, tired of being unable to come up to his conception of Léocadia, makes this charge: "So there: you are young, rich, handsome, and your peas- ant's hands are not hard . . . You should try to live, to be happy and to forget this story, because, I really believe, Monsieur, that you, too, never really loved her" (4th tabl.). Ultimately Albert comes to this admission himself, but not first without offering the explanation of his comedy. His comedy—not his aunt's. For hers is one he consents to play in only because it makes his own pos- sible. In a long tirade which anticipates the Sartrean Kean's de- scription of the audience as a pack of *oisifs,* Albert explains to Amanda that he finds the world to be a "fog of boredom" in which most people fabricate for themselves the most naive, frivo- lous, and futile pretexts as means of ignoring the absurdity of existence: alcohol, boy-scout heroism, work, Swedish gymnastics, addiction to sports, the rational cultivation of pleasure, etc. Albert disdained most of these dodges and felt adrift in the world until Léocadia appeared. "But this madwoman with her ridiculous re- finement, her frivolities, she was intelligence itself, mademoi- selle . . ." And Albert proceeds to exalt this goddess of intelli- gence who had taught him to play at life. But to Léocadia's play of intelligence Amanda simply counters her play of the flesh. She

remains absolutely unmoved by Albert's passionate tirade and
walks off his stage, leaving him to his fellow actor, the café host
of his Léocadia days, whom he quaveringly asks: "You have never
doubted, have you, that I loved her more than anything in the
world?"

Amanda stops acting. When she meets Albert the following
morning in the beauty of a dawn which already suggests that we
will be turning away from the dream concerns of the night before,
she steers him away from his old haunts. She makes him sit on the
terrace in the sunlight and not indoors next to the artificial
warmth of the fire at a table he had shared with Léocadia. She
makes him eat a real breakfast of coffee and bread, refusing him
his customary Léocadian beverage of lemonade. And she makes
him realize that he is in love with her, not with Léocadia—in spite
of his shouted protests to the contrary: "If you didn't love me,
you wouldn't be shouting so loud . . . Oh! please, don't torment
yourself any more with this dream where everything slips through
your fingers. See how the world around you is full of sure things,
flowers one can smell, grass which you can take and rub in your
hands . . ." (5th tabl.). And Albert, as if to test her "philosophy
of the hands," embraces Amanda—and succumbs. "How simple
it is, it's true. How easy it is. How sure!"

Triumph of reality over illusion? Edward Owen Marsh believes
so: "In *Léocadia* reality triumphs and the dream is justly shat-
tered. It is a decisive victory—the victory of reality in fact means
a rejection of the impossible and an acceptance of the real
world." [1] But have we not once again the triumph of reality in an
illusion? For Amanda succeeds in replacing Léocadia only as an
actress in spite of herself: in the play which has been arranged by
the duchess. Only when she thinks that she has stopped playing
does Amanda really begin to play the role the duchess has hired
her for. *Léocadia* ends as the duchess, hunting with the Baron
Hector, knocks down an extravagant bird, "a funny sort of bird,
whose feathers are too long. It clings to everything, [yet] its legs
are too long, it doesn't know where to settle down." Symbol of
Léocadia, of course: "Poor Léocadia!" the duchess goes on, "she
was reduced to strangling herself with her beautiful scarf and
there we've killed her a second time in his memory. We had to
save our little Albert. And if it's the young Amandas who save the

little Alberts, then long live the Amandas!" (5th tabl.) Playing
herself, Amanda has been the unwitting marionette of the duchess. The triumph of reality in illusion has been genuine enough,
but it has been unconscious. For the deliberate assumption of the
stage in the name of the natural we must look to the later Anouilh.

In *L'Invitation au château* (1947) Anouilh has reinforced his
play theme by the twin theme. Horace, the sardonic, cerebral
twin, hires Isabelle, a young dancer and sometimes seamstress, to
play up to his sentimental twin, Frédéric, during a ball in the
family castle. Horace himself intends to play up to Isabelle (mistress, by the way, of Romainville, a sycophantic man of the world
living off the twins' aunt, Mme Desmermortes). He hopes thereby
to force Diana, his brother's fianceé, whom he loves and whom he
knows to be in love with himself, to reveal in her jealousy the
vicious, immoral side of her to which her fiancé is blinded. The
play over, Frédéric can console himself with the discovery of
truth; Isabelle, paid off with the fancy party dress, can go back to
her sewing or dancing; Horace can go off with Diana. But Isabelle complicates things by falling in love with Horace. She agrees
to play the game of making love to Frédéric only because in the
twin she can find the image of his brother.

In a bewildering set of entries and exits (the twins are played
by one actor) Horace's little comedy nearly comes off. But Isabelle's sincerity gets the best of her; rejected by Horace, frustrated
by her paradoxical nearness to him through her love-making to
Frédéric, taunted by the spiteful Diana, she breaks down. "I have
loved only you," she cries to Horace through tears, "while I have
been playing this horrible masquerade. Playing? No, for it was
you I really made love to in the image of Frédéric." But it is not
Horace who has suddenly entered to receive the full blast of her
tirade—it is Frédéric. Nevertheless, in this unwitting address, as
in the deliberate illusion of her masquerade, Isabelle is speaking
to the man she loves. This truth of the seemingly only apparent
truth of the comedy arranged by Horace does not become clear
until the comedy arranged by his aunt is played. Apprised of
Horace's "play" by her ex-actress lady in waiting, who no more
than Hamlet's actors can "keep counsel," Mme Desmermortes
arranges for Isabelle and Frédéric to walk in the garden where
they can complain to each other over the trick played upon them.

Mme Desmermortes knows that in five minutes the two will discover the truth of her analysis of Isabelle's relationship to the twins: "With them, what's convenient is that you always have the other under hand. It's not Horace you love, my dear, it's his image. And, if you are unhappy this evening, if you've wanted to throw yourself fully dressed into my pools, it's because you have confusedly felt that there was nothing for you behind that image" (v). With Horace and Diana, however, "the comedy begins to wear a little thin." The aunt is provoked to this complaint by Horace' refusal to go after the rich Diana "because everyone will believe it's the father's money I'm in love with." Fortunately, Mme Desmermortes is provided by fate with an actor whose sincerity plays right into her hands. Diana's father, Messerchmann, has attempted to give up the false, illusory happiness of wealth by "dumping" all of his holdings. Horace then agrees to accept an impoverished Diana.

Once again, then, we have in an Anouilh play the triumph of reality in illusion (and once again the aunt's illusion, not the nephew's). In *L'Invitation* the triumph is amusingly reinforced by the final incident of the play: Messerchmann learns that his sincere dumping of his stocks has not impoverished him at all. The move, countered by his competitors as a ruse, has made him twice as rich.

In the four plays considered so far, Anouilh's use of the play within a play has been figurative. The impromptus which Lady Hurf, Georges, the duchess, Horace, and his aunt put on are playlike, not formal plays. It is the impromptu character of these near plays which most easily lends them to the theme of the breakdown of illusion and reality. But, to recall our eighteenth-century formula, there is no retroactive formalization of the action. In *La Répétition* (1950) Anouilh offers a true play within a play, a pretense involving both impersonation and formality, thus posing for himself a more difficult challenge: the breakdown of the admittedly formal. Tigre and his fellow "comédiens de société" put on, appropriately enough considering their amateur status, a Marivaux play, *La Double Inconstance*. Through an ingenious matching of tone between inner and outer play, with the actors appearing throughout in play costumes and in the setting of the eighteenth-century château Tigre and his wife are presumed to

have inherited, Anouilh meets the challenge. He manages to keep
the audience of *La Répétition* wondering when it is a Marivaux
and when an Anouilh reply it is hearing.

It is more than a question of tone and costuming, of course.
Tigre in his staging of the Marivaux play is responsible for a good
deal of the *marivaudage* by his assignation of roles. Much of the
pleasure he finds in putting on the play is in the opportunity it
affords him to make sport of his friends.

> HORTENSIA (*Tigre's mistress*): I do not doubt it. That's
> what love is. I've loved in the same way. And I can recog-
> nize myself in this business of the little ball. (*To Tigre*): Is
> she sincere in saying that? I feel that I am speaking falsely.
> Was she really in love? Did she one day prefer a little ball of
> wool to all the jewels the prince offered her?
> TIGRE: And you, my dear Hortensia?
> HORTENSIA: Tigre, it's not a question of me. If this is a
> game you are playing, it is not funny. You just said that we
> were not ourselves . . .
> TIGRE: Excuse me. When I handed out the roles, I knew
> just what I was doing. You gave your lines perfectly.
> HORTENSIA: I gave them "with sincerity."
> TIGRE: And since you have never preferred the slightest
> ball of wool to your own pleasure, in giving your line "with
> sincerity" you sounded abominably false. It was perfect. It
> was what I wanted. Go on.

Subjectivity, as we learned from Molière, is a factor which the
director of a play must sometimes take into account in his efforts
to objectify the work. Tigre counts on Hortensia's absolute inability to be anybody but her own insincere self. She is, as he says,
perfect then for creating in the play Flaminia in all the "sincerity"
of her falseness.

But it would be a misconception to push the Molière parallel
too far in the case of Tigre. Though he may have a reputation for
objectivity and detachment, on this occasion his intentions are
anything but objective. For if his play is to benefit from the sincerity of his fellow actors, it will do so, too, from the fact that, as
the prince, his love-making to Lucile-Sylvia will be quite genuine.
Indeed, it is questionable whether he even thinks as much about

the requirements of the illusion when he is onstage as Hortensia does. Like the prince he plays, Tigre is only playing at playing a role: the prince, we remember, pretends to Sylvia that he is a mere soldier in order to be able to make love to the charming girl from the lower classes with whom he has fallen in love. And, in so playing for serious purposes, Tigre, like the prince, is being unfaithful to the ladies of his court, Hortensia and his wife Eliane.

Tigre's is not the only double inconstancy in *La Répétition*, however, nor is he the only *metteur-en-scène*. Victimized by the formal maze of Tigre's play, Hortensia and Eliane plot two informal countercomedies. The first, in which Eliane pretends to lose a valuable emerald in order to be able to oust Lucile on a charge of theft, fails. The ruse is too patently theatrical for the theatrically sophisticated Tigre not to see through it. The second, however, succeeds. Tigre is lured away by a typically theatrical urgent telegram (we shall return to this theatrical trick) and Héro, Tigre's best friend and a coward, seduces Lucile by telling her that Tigre, tired of the little comedy with her and feeling himself to be the victim of his own illusion, has asked Héro to take Lucile off his hands.

Tigre and Lucile pay the price of living in illusion only: being shocked and hurt when the play comes to an end. Tigre is—or was—according to his wife one of the last men of this age to understand "that one must take futility seriously." Having fallen in love with Lucile, however, Tigre sees what lay behind this serious futility: "This line of my life—so gracious and so clean— from my first cotillion ball to my presidency of the Jockey Club twenty years from now, at my funeral, with all of Paris in mourning clothes, I've just realized, would be undoubtedly the nice subject of an article in *Figaro*—and nothing for me. I didn't know before why I used to be so gay: I was bored" (Act v). But he comes out of this maze of futility in which he alone knew his way only to find himself in quite another maze where he does not: Eliane's second comedy. One might object that it is ridiculous that Tigre should be so trapped: as the sophisticated Tigre saw through the patently theatrical ruse of the hidden gem, so he should have seen through the patently theatrical ruse of the urgent telegram. But this is to miss the essential irony of the play; the theatrically sophisticated Tigre is meant to fall victim to his wife's stratagem.

Just as Hortensia in her acting is really more objectively concerned with the play than is Tigre in his, so Eliane sees more clearly through his play than he does through hers; Eliane sees that her husband is really in love with Lucile just as she sees to what extent his love has blinded him. Unwittingly, he has "primed himself for the kill."

Why does the stratagem of the wire succeed and not that of the emerald? The question is vain, though it can be answered with *vraisemblance* that the telegram is less evidently Eliane's doing. If it were not the telegram, it would have been some other stratagem: the irony of the situation demands that he be fooled in this theatrical way. But should not Tigre have been all the more suspicious of a telegram, following the incident of the emerald? Possibly, if Tigre were living by the head, instead of by the heart. It is Eliane who is living by intelligence, that goddess much deprecated in Anouilh's theater, and to be a success as an actress one needs much more head than heart.

For Tigre, "le coeur est la dupe de l'esprit." As it is also for Lucile, who is closer to the fragile Isabelle of *L'Invitation* than she is to the assertive Amanda of *Léocadia*. Like Tigre, Lucile attempts to make her sincerity the basis of her *jeu*. Like him, she is only pretending at insincerity in the Marivaux comedy; she is being real in an illusion: she uses the role for the communication of her own feelings. She would have the play be a stratagem—she will find it to be a maze. She shares Tigre's new-found single standard, she wants to be herself outside of the play as well. But to be everywhere the same, Eliane and Héro make her realize, is to have a double standard: one rule for herself and Tigre, another for Eliane and Héro. If Lucile attempts to turn the tables by seeking reality in illusion (the Marivaux play), they'll turn them on her and give her illusion in reality (Héro's lie). Lucile has placed her head at the service of her heart—and lost. Intelligence is not her strong point. If success for her in the inner play depends on an esthetic of identification, so, too, does the play of life—as Eliane knows and Lucile does not. The difference is that the Marivaux play, as we have seen, depends on a fundamental good faith; Eliane's "play" on a fundamental bad faith. Eliane is as much herself in her treachery as Lucile and Tigre in their sincerity.

So the pièce rose of Tigre becomes the pièce noire of Eliane;

The Rehearsal becomes *Love Punished* (the subtitle of the play). The shattering note from the departed Lucile proves to Tigre that if he wants to live in the real world it must be with the Elianes not with the Luciles. Disillusioned, Tigre himself departs. To search for Lucile? He knows better: he will not find her, for Lucile's is a tragic departure. Exile, as Racine's *Bérénice* teaches us, is as telling a symbol of tragedy as death or blinding. The separation of the lovers is a final representation of the irreparable split between appearance and reality which is the lesson of the whole play. It is only in appearance, in the illusion of the Marivaux play, that Lucile and Tigre could find each other. In reality, they must remain forever apart. The person's efforts to use the *persona* fail—as they were bound to. For one comedy only sets up another; reality, Tigre and Lucile discover most ruefully, is theatrical with a vengeance. They could love each other sincerely only in some idyllic dream world where their love would be beyond the challenge of the Elianes and the Héros. Society is, by definition, dramatic; "all the world's a stage," a scene of conflict, and conflict inevitably involves ruse. Sincerity exists only beyond the conflict, that is, off the stage. Thus, like most of the pièces noires, *La Répétition* proves the partial truth of Robert Champigny's contention that in Anouilh, "the theatre aspires to commit suicide." [2] But generalizing thus, Champigny forgets his own earlier insight that "in some of his plays, generally *pièces roses* or *brillantes,* no rupture is indicated between theatre and 'real' life." [3] In these plays, as in Molière, reality triumphs *in* illusion; life is seen not as limitation but as possibility; the vision is rose. If in *La Répétition* Eliane makes Tigre an actor in spite of himself and things turn out for the worse, we must remember that in *Léocadia* the duchess makes Amanda an actress in spite of herself and things turn out for the best.

In *Colombe* (1951) Anouilh succeeds in capturing the two aspects of his vision, the rose of *Léocadia* and the noir of *La Répétition* in a single dramatic image. In contrast to all of the plays we have examined thus far, Anouilh now uses the professional theater as the setting of his action: a real theater and not a castle theater, real actors and not amateur actors. In *Colombe,* too, he now reverses his earlier procedure and uses life as a focus through which to look at the theater (ultimately, of course, it is a vision of life which is sought in both procedures). It is not so much Julien who brings Colombe into the theater world as Colombe who brings Julien into that world, or back into it, as they go to his actress-mother's loge in order to receive help for his little family now that he is going into the service.

Now, only such a need could bring Julien into the theater he detests as a living lie. For him the theater has meant only loneliness and abandonment, the isolation of his bastardy doubled by the isolation of being the child of a famous actress. The only tenderness his mother has ever shown him has been the phony affection of publicity photographs. Nor is the image of Mme Alexandra, when we first meet her backstage in this antiquated, 1910 atmosphere, intended to compensate for her son's garish and cruel portrait of her. Surrounded by her general staff of hairdressers, theater directors, pedicurists, and what have you, she walks right by her son and his wife without even looking at them in order to pass into her loge, "yapping in that voice deformed by the false teeth which have helped to make her glory." Throughout the first act, indeed, Anouilh states Julien's case in its most extreme form: not only Mme Alexandra but all of the people of her entourage are as black, as false, as lecherous, as cowardly, as outlandish, as vicious, as self-centered—in sum, as despicable—as Julien makes them out to be to Colombe.

Or at least they seem all of these things from the vantage of Julien's world, "a world where everything is more difficult and purer," the world which the sweet Colombe represents to him. But in Colombe's gentle resistance to Julien's excited denigration of the theater, one senses that Anouilh is stating another case. When Julien refuses to allow her to like his brother Armand precisely because the latter is "gentil" whereas he is not, Colombe protests:

> COLOMBE: Oh, it's not yours to boast about. It's rather a quality to be nice.
> JULIEN (*shouts*): No!
> COLOMBE (*with a comical sigh*): How complicated everything is with you, my sweet! I always have to be on guard. And for me, everything is so simple . . . Everyone is nice, nothing is ugly, and I want only to be happy . . . (*She day-*

dreams a bit and sighs): Happy . . . It's funny, it's a word
which tickles the lips when you say it, as if someone were
kissing you.   (Act 1)

Everybody is nice—even the people of this world in which, to
generalize Armand's description of his mother's dressing room,
"everything is rigorously false."

Or perhaps, as suggested by Colombe's further adventures in
the theater world to which she herself now belongs as a bit actress:
especially people of this world are nice. For it is the people of this
supposedly false world who really appreciate Colombe's natural
charm with a justice that the more honest Julien could never
muster. To be sure, they are all after something from Colombe—
but what they are after is precisely the fresh, young charm which
is the essence of Colombe. Besides, Colombe's innocence is not
without wile: she knows how to handle the flibbertigibbet Poète-
Chéri, the ridiculously overconfident actor du Bartas, the overeager but ever-ready-to-pay theater director, Desfournettes. The
spirit of the action as Colombe wards off the advances of these
backstage Lotharios is good-natured and lighthearted, and Julien,
if we remember him at all, is made to seem by contrast a pompous
ass. But with the appearance of Armand we are made to wonder
if Colombe's wile is without innocence. After all, Colombe invites Armand, not he her, to rehearse the love scene of the play
she is to appear in, a rehearsal in which Armand makes love to
her.

Which Colombe, Julien asks, was the true one: the innocent
Colombe of the first act or the wily Colombe of the second? Julien, armed with an accusing letter from La Surette, the stage manager, also wants to know. The third act is a masterful interweaving
of the deceitful and the innocent. Colombe's naive reassurances
to Julien in her dressing room are punctuated by the compromis-
ing intrusions of her friends and Julien's enemies, the members
of Mme Alexandra's troupe. "Onstage for the first act," cries La
Surette as he leaves Julien hidden, in traditional cuckold fashion,
in the closet of Colombe's dressing room. But when Julien, unable
because of his pathetic sincerity to play this deceitful role, steps
out of the closet in order to confront Colombe with his accusa-
tions, the act which begins goes on behind the dressing room

door, not on the stage. In an ironic reversal of roles, the spectators
of the action are the actors of the troupe, who stand glued to the
outer side of the door. Occasionally some of them become actors
in the dressing room drama, with most comitragic results:

> JULIEN: You know very well what I mean. Don't play in-
> nocent.
> COLOMBE (*luminous*): But no, my sweet, I know nothing.
> (*Du Bartas leaves his room half dressed and goes to knock at
> Colombe's door.*)
> DU BARTAS: Toc! Toc! Are you there, my little kitten? I
> wanted to tell you to pay strict attention. (*He opens the door
> and sees Julien*): Oh, Pardon me!   (III)

Several such damning juxtapositions of tarnish and luminosity
pile up throughout the act against Colombe: in another amusing
interruption she asks Julien his opinion of the costly suit we know
Desfournettes to have promised her on his usual conditions; in an
outburst of delighted mockery she tells Julien that he should see
Poète-Chéri in his underwear and when Julien reacts menacingly
to the image, Colombe compounds her fault by claiming that it is
with du Bartas that she "merely discusses" such intimate matters;
Colombe admits to having dined with the oversolicitous coiffeur;
she has, she admits, gone into Desfournettes's office fully aware of
his reputation, etc., etc. Julien can only slap her face in a rage of
despair and jealousy: "Whore! Lousy little whore like all the
others. I'll have his hide, that one's!" And, as Colombe collapses
into the faint of outraged innocence and Julien races to find
Desfournettes, Mme Alexandra decides it is time to act: she calls
for the curtain on the real play, "La Maréchale d'amour." Upon
which Colombe, the crushed, the outraged, the tear-stricken Colombe "comes to, miraculously. She goes to the mirror and asks:
'My hair is not too mussed?' " And the *habilleuse* having told her
the simple truth—"non"—Colombe goes off to put on her costume. The play begins and Julien is left alone in his wife's dressing room. Suddenly Armand, gay, nonchalant, debonair Armand,
the cliché *garçon de joie* of the tinsel and glitter theater world,
appears, "un petit bouquet à la main." Julien suddenly realizes
that Armand is Colombe's lover. Humble before Julien in a way
that Colombe had not been, Armand begs that Julien strike him.

But Julien refuses, he wants only to understand: he embraces Armand in just the way he imagines Colombe to have done. The kiss only deepens his incomprehension.

Morally speaking the third act, apparently like the first, belongs to Julien: Colombe is a treacherous little hypocrite. It is this view of her which the outlandish play within a play at the beginning of Act IV seems to confirm. In the concluding scenes of "La Maréchale d'amour" Colombe is the very picture of innocence and charm as she plays the ingénue to Mme Alexandra's maréchale, but this innocence and charm must be set in the context of her admitted infidelities to Julien. The inner play evidently is satirical and certain critics have wondered if it is not Anouilh's satire of contemporary tendencies in the French theater. But it would be difficult to indicate just what tendencies, for the flamboyant verses, the *style outré* of the gestures, the ridiculous sentimentality of the figures seem more a parody of nineteenth-century melodrama than of any modern tendency. The setting of *Colombe* itself is rather archaic, as I have said. Historical *vraisemblance,* then? It is more likely, as with the dating, a question of poetic truth: the satire is aimed at the actors of the play within a play and, through them, at the theater itself. Backstage we have seen Mme Alexandra in all the decaying glory of the aging actress; onstage she is the young maréchale, pursued by a young and elegant officer, played, naturally, by that aging, bumbling Lothario, du Bartas. Again, the noble maréchal, the husband who places honor of country above personal honor, is played by La Surette, whose conceptions of honor, personal and otherwise, we can judge from his poisonous letter to Julien. Only Colombe, who is as luminously innocent onstage as she was backstage in her tearful breakdown before the enraged Julien, seems suited to her role. "Madame, he will come back and he will be faithful," is Colombe's only line in the scene, the only line of the Colombe whose conception of fidelity we must judge from the scene with Julien.

The play within a play, then, captures in a single dramatic image those two moments, those two images which have only alternated for us in the play up to this time: the superficial and the profound, the illusory and the real, the false and the true—Mme Alexandra and the others in their patent, theatrical charm and Colombe in her patent but natural charm.

For it is a naturally innocent and charming Colombe who appears on the stage both in and outside of the play within a play—
as the final encounter between her and Julien proves to us. Significantly, like the first encounter, which we shall discuss in a
moment, it occurs on the stage where Colombe has just completed
her role as Clorinde, but now a stage gradually denuded by the
stagehands even as she and Julien quarrel. To the Julien who
self-pityingly and at great length tells her that he knows all about
her and Armand, Colombe, still costumed as Clorinde, listens
quietly and enigmatically. Finally she asks Julien if he would
not prefer for her sake to continue while she is redressing in her
loge, as she is in a hurry to keep an engagement which will mean
much to her career. His heart is breaking, yet she is thinking only
about a professional appointment! Julien explodes, accusing her
in the most bitter tones of a fall from moral grace. But Colombe
reminds him of her fall from another kind of grace, the grace of
living: "Why is it you who would always know what was beautiful? What's beautiful is what one loves. And me, I loved the street
singers' songs, dancing, pretty dresses, bouquets of flowers. But
you never bought anything" (IV). With his imperious moral sensibility, Julien, to recall a famous Gidean formula in this debate
about kinds of sincerity, "ankylose la vie" ("ossifies life"). Julien,
who could not find Colombe's meaning in the concrete gesture of
a kiss, will never escape the prison of his *vision noire* through the
secondary reality of words. One view of life confronts another;
Julien can only continue to accuse Colombe of insincerity. Why,
he wants to know, did she greet him with such a warm embrace
upon his return that evening? She tells him gently that she was
glad to see him. Besides, "it was so stupid what you were thinking.
Besides, I wasn't going to tell you yes . . . nor tell you the truth
either, in order to hurt you still more. I do love you, you were
leaving tomorrow, I was afraid that you might have troubles all
alone, back there. I would have preferred that you not know right
away" (IV). She can only reply to him from the serenity of her
vision rose: she lies to him not to do him harm but to spare him
harm. More than this: in order to bring him good, the good of her
body, for Colombe's, like Amanda's of *Léocadia,* is a "philosophy
of the hands."

It is, of course, a philosophy which Julien does not understand.

Above her tender reminiscences of their earlier happiness, Julien
only screeches: "What about Armand? Did you enjoy making love
to him too?" More exasperated than ruffled, Colombe can only
reply: "Armand, too. Only, it's not the same, that's all. You have
a genius for complicating everything, you!" (IV) Julien nostalgically prefers his Colombe of two years ago. But that Colombe, the
present one tells him, never existed. The little flower girl had
been too long in the business before Julien met her for that
Colombe of his ever to have had a chance to be born. There had
been too many marriage feasts where the father-in-law had invited
the little flower girl to share his "bed of flowers"; too many burial
services where one bereaved cousin had managed to overcome his
grief sufficiently to use Colombe's shoulder as a pillow; too many
trips to the shop cellar required by the florist, ever eager to accompany Colombe there. "Keep her, if you want to, your sugar-
doll Colombe, but that saintly little ninny, you have dreamed her
just like all the rest, my poor pet" (IV).

Like the Georges of *Le Rendez-vous*, Julien has his "ideal
family"; like the Albert of *Léocadia*, his ideal mistress. This fact
is of the utmost importance in interpreting the paradoxical
prologue-as-epilogue with which Colombe concludes, for it reminds us that Julien's innocent Colombe is not necessarily *the*
innocent Colombe. This flashback which is also the fade-out of
the action is not a mere display of virtuosity on Anouilh's part,
as some commentators have believed. Rather: "It is torture
[Marsh writes] for him to think that her love for him may never
have been real, that all he has lived for was without foundation.
This is the point on which the whole play revolves, and that is
why the last scene—a dreamlike evocation of their first meeting,
on the empty stage, when they fall in love—is an overwhelming
climax, not just an appended flashback. Dramatically it brings
bewilderment to the highest pitch of intensity and underlines all
the conflicting truths about Colombe which Julien will never
understand." [4] This comes closer to the true genius of Anouilh's
unusual structure. But the paradox of the evocation of this early
Colombe is not contained in the question Marsh goes on to pose:
"Which was the real Colombe? And if the second is real, was the
first not so?" [5] The paradox is not that we have had two Colombes,
but one all along. Or, to state the same truth somewhat differ-

ently, the answer to each of Marsh's two questions—Was the first Colombe real? Was the second real?—is yes. Let us look in some detail at the strange structure which provides this single answer to both questions.

The flashback is Anouilh's final technical solution to the problem of projecting his double vision of life as not "rose ou noir" but "rose *et* noir." It is a parallel structure to the earlier play within a play of *Colombe* and, played as it is on the same stage, it is deliberately playlike in its paradoxical presentation of an actual event. The flashback is rose because it recalls to Julien the innocent creature with whom he had fled the theater and its noir two years ago; but because it is past, only a dream to Julien, it is noir, a negative reminder of the real fact that Colombe has returned to the theater. It is black, too, being a dream looking to a future embittered by the past. But Julien's relationship to the flashback apart, the flashback is rose et noir within itself, for as much as it is a dream the flashback is a reality. In it we do not see a fantasy Colombe whom Julien constructs out of whole cloth; we see Colombe both as she was two years ago in reality and as she is now.

For the qualities which led the people of Mme Alexandra's world to invite Colombe into that world after her marriage to Julien are the same qualities which led those people to invite her into their world before the marriage. Colombe in the flashback is the same charming, fresh, natural creature of the rest of the play. The Colombe who in Act IV defends before a scowling Julien the grace of living is the same Colombe who in the flashback defends Julien against the ungracious brutality of the troupe. On each occasion her motive is the same: the only evil in life, according to Colombe (and, somewhat more solemnly, to Albert Schweitzer), is to do harm to life. Colombe is etymologically innocent—Latin *innocens,* "not hurtful"; her defense of Julien is spontaneous, natural, innocent. To the Julien who thinks he has gained an ally against the theater by virtue of it, Colombe says, "You mustn't thank me. I didn't even do it deliberately. When they wanted to run you off, that hurt me inside of me. I cried out. And then, I found myself in your arms. It's too fast, isn't it? it isn't serious?" (IV) It has been so fast that she has not been aware that her good deed has cost her the part in the play she was to get (the role of an innocent flower girl). However, "cost" with its implications of hypocrisy is an inappropriate category for discussing Colombe. She is not a Léocadia, "an extravagant bird," but she is, as her name tells us, a dove. She had as guilelessly agreed to try out for the part as she later guilelessly leaped to Julien's defense. When he leads her out of the theater, Julien is not preventing Colombe's entry into the life of the theater; he is postponing it.

The dream flashback is epilogue to the structure, prologue to the action, analogue to the inner play. In the prologue-epilogue, as in the inner play, Colombe is an ingénue. The theater with its changing visages is the ideal calling for her whose commitment to the lovely flexibility of life reminds us of Gide's exhortation to "readiness" ("disponibilité"). As she dances in the playlike dream flashback of Act IV, she recaptures for us that vision which Molière offered in the concluding ballet of *Le Malade:* life is a masked ballet where we find ourselves in the successive personages (or persons, to recall for the last time the common Latin root) we become. If the theater is a frightening maze to Julien, for Colombe it is a fascinating maze of mirrors, in which she delights in the new view of herself which each turn in the maze brings. "It's me . . . it's me . . ." she had murmured ecstatically as she contemplated herself in the mirror wearing her first costume (I). But the maze conception is too negative to express Colombe's view of the theater. The play is rather a kaleidoscope, a succession of brilliant, multicolored images, each to be enjoyed for its own sake, no single one to be regretted when passed. The play as kaleidoscope brings to a term Anouilh's vision rose. But in the reality of the playlike dream, as in the illusion of the play within a play, Colombe is not the only one to dance. There are the others in their unmistakable blackness: the aging young maréchale and hardhearted mother Alexandra; the elegant young officer and lecherous Lothario du Bartas; the honorable maréchal and treacherous stage manager La Surette. If Colombe, ingenuous offstage as on, represents half of the paradox of the theater—its nearness and resemblance to life—Mme Alexandra and the others, leading obviously "theatrical" and disingenuous lives, represent the other half for us—its distance and dissociation from life. Colombe's pièce rose, the life of the theater, is Julien's pièce noire, thus bringing to a term the other aspect of Anouilh's vision.

Both aspects are presented in a single structural metaphor. *Colombe* is at once a tragicomedy and a comitragedy. "Mais je l'aime," Julien laments to his mother after Colombe has left him. Mme Alexandra says, "Fine! That's a fact. But she doesn't love you any longer. That's another fact, just as valid as the first" (IV). One fact confronts another; one view of life confronts another. For Julien there is an unclosable breach in reality between the apparent and the true; for Colombe the succeeding appearances are all true. It is wrong to speak, as Radine does, of Anouilh's concessions to the public through the happy endings of some of his plays.[6] (At the heart of such a criticism lies the same point of view which would treat Molière's comédies-ballets as minor works.) Anouilh simply recognizes the equal validity of two possible responses to the human condition: the tragic and the comic. Is his a diluted or confused vision, then? The dogmatic polarization which such a question implies denies the very essence of Anouilh's double vision. The playwright is not asking us to choose, nor is he choosing for us one or the other response. He is not teaching us a lesson but offering us a description. The comic and the tragic are not dogmas in Anouilh. They are temptations. They are the states of being between which man forever oscillates.

Postface

IT IS USUAL in this "age of Pirandello" to rank Anouilh high on the list of those who have come under the influence of the great Italian spellbinder. Yet the compliment is not only left-handed, it is inappropriate. Theatrical self-consciousness, expressing itself frequently in the form of a play within a play, is not enough to label a dramatist Pirandellian—and, as I hope this essay has proved, this includes Pirandello himself. What counts is the view of reality the dramatist embodies through this form. On this score, the differences between Pirandello and Anouilh stand forth much more clearly than the resemblances. For example, contrary to the Ponza-Frolas, Anouilh's sympathetic characters, compelled by an existentialist need for sincerity, refuse those "remedies for life's ills" which Pirandellian compassion finds in self-avowed lying and other forms of consciously accepted illusion. However, if in spite of Anouilh's obvious individuality, we must, at the risk of obscuring his genius, capture him in an influence, it is perhaps better to start at home in the case of this deeply French writer. I have already pointed to the *marivaudage* of many of the early plays and, on occasion, the later Anouilh seems to arrive at some conception of the theater akin to that of the late Molière. As for more contemporary echoes in his work, Anouilh, like most of his generation, seems to have been more deeply impressed with Gide's notions of sincerity and openness to experience than he has with Pirandello's related notions of the tragic complexity of existence and the need for self-deception.

In its uniqueness, its failure simply to tag along like most contemporary theater about the theater in the wake of Pirandello, Anouilh's work serves as a welcome caution to those who believe that the formula of the play within a play comes to some kind of genetic fulfillment in Pirandello and has now only to wither on the vine of imitation or fall into desuetude like some vestigial organ. The device lies at hand, ever ready to be renewed by the unpredictable genius of individual poetic vision.

Or, more generally, of artistic vision, for the play within a play is but one example of the much larger phenomenon of artistic self-consciousness. It would be interesting to study self-conscious conceptions of the creative act in the other arts or in other literary forms. In my Molière discussion I suggested a parallel conception in Vermeer's *The Painter's Art*. Other parallels will occur to the reader: like Corneille directing from within the center of his creation the action of *L'Illusion comique,* there is Veronese standing dramatically in the center of *Christ in the House of Levi* (competing, indeed, for the spectator's attention with Christ himself); like Genest his own executioner and Rotrou his own judge in *Le Véritable Saint Genest* there is Caravaggio, his own executioner as he portrays himself in the head of Goliath held by the victorious David. In the early nineteenth century one is struck by the number of self-portraits by painters in which there is little or no evidence that the man who so proudly challenges the spectator is, in fact, a painter. On the other hand, as one draws closer to the esthetically preoccupied artists of the twentieth century— the century of the play as a kind of workshop—one is struck by a reversal of interest: not the man as such but the painter as such is the subject (for example, the numerous studio studies of Matisse).[1]

The question of intercalated form is an especially interesting one in the novel. One thinks of the "framed" stories of Boccaccio and Marguerite de Navarre, of course. And it has been said by one critic that *Don Quixote,* the first novel, is a book about books,[2] so that it is not surprising that there should be within it many tales within tales. At the heart of the striking originality of Diderot's *Jacques le fataliste* lies the author's preoccupation with the problem of presentation not only of Jacques's story but of any story. Nearer to our own times one thinks of the infinite involutions of Proust's great novel and of the concentric structure of the *récits* of Gide, a writer for whom the *composition en abyme* is truly an obsession, one finding supreme satisfaction in *Les Faux-Monnayeurs.*

But here "the play within a play's the thing." Though I would not violate the individuality of a single dramatist I have considered, certain affinities among their differing conceptions of the theater can be noted. The early Shakespeare, Corneille, Molière, Marivaux, Sartre, Anouilh—these suppose a view of the play as simply play; they lean heavily, some immediately, others ultimately, on the principle of dissociation. Rotrou, Legouvé, Dumas, Pirandello, Schnitzler, sometimes Anouilh—these suppose a view of the play as more than a play; they lean heavily on the principle of identification. In the plays giving rise to these various conceptions I hope I have come to an essential truth about the work. I would not, however, contend—particularly in the case of Shakespeare or Corneille or Molière—that I have come to *the* essential truth. If my essay on an individual dramatist has placed too great an emphasis on a single aspect of his work, I do not deny the importance of other aspects or impugn the validity of other ways of getting at any or all aspects of the work in question . . .

else my project fails,
Which was to please.
The Tempest (Epilogue)

Appendix

Résumés of Chief Continental Plays before Schnitzler's *The Green Cockatoo*

I HAVE limited this appendix as indicated, feeling that the reader would undoubtedly be familiar with the plays of Shakespeare and with Molière's famous *Malade imaginaire*. As for the plays of Schnitzler, Pirandello, and Anouilh, I have found it more convenient to incorporate the résumés in my discussion in order to demonstrate the peculiar fusion of illusion and reality which marks these plays as conceptions of the theater characteristic of the twentieth century.

1. Rotrou, *Le Véritable Saint Genest*

Valérie, daughter of the Emperor Dioclétien, tells a confidant of her misgivings about a dream in which she found herself married to a lowly shepherd. While the young women discuss the dream, Maximin, the emperor's commander in the East, arrives. Dioclétien has already raised Maximin to equal authority with himself and he now further honors him by giving him his daughter in marriage, thereby gloriously capping the new coemperor's rise from lowly shepherd as well as making his daughter's dream come true. To celebrate the marriage, Dioclétien summons the actor Genest to perform. After a discussion in which many familiar works are rejected, the actor agrees to play "The Martyrdom of Adrien," the hero of this dramatic biography being a former officer of Maximin who was converted to Christianity. Backstage, as Genest prepares for the play, the lines he rehearses mysteriously disturb him. His anxiety is increased when he believes he hears a voice telling him he will not imitate "in vain." More puzzled than convinced, he goes on. In the inner play, one Flavie reminds the former officer, Adrien, of his indebtedness to Maximin, but the converted pagan, reviewing the sources of his new belief, re-jects all pleas to recant. Impressed deeply, the offstage emperors hasten backstage to congratulate Genest on the force of his act-ing. After some offstage discussion, we return to the inner play: Natalie, Adrien's wife, visits the new convert in prison. She re-veals that she, too, is a Christian, but must keep it a secret, as this appears to be God's will. Genest interrupts the play at this point to complain of a disturbance by a rowdy crowd and when the play resumes we see Adrien about to receive from the emperor a final chance to recant. His wife mistakes his position and berates him as an apostate. However, Adrien succeeds in reassuring her and then prepares to receive baptism. As the character Adrien turns to the divine light which symbolizes his "baptism of fire," he be-comes the converted actor, Genest. The actor steps out of his role, to the confusion and disbelief of the other actors and specta-tors. Finally taking Genest at his word that he has literally been converted to Christianity, the emperors have him seized. The other actors, now themselves suspect, quickly absolve themselves, but plead nonetheless for Genest to the emperors. But, refusing to recant, Genest goes to his own martyrdom. While the emperors scorn, the actors lament their dead comrade.

2. Corneille, *L'Illusion comique*

Dorante brings his friend Pridamant to the grotto of Alcandre, a magician, hoping to learn something about Clindor, the son whom Pridamant admits to having unjustly banished. Alcandre evokes for the father the image of his son in the service of the braggart captain, Matamore, whom Clindor is deceiving by pur-suing Isabelle, Matamore's intended. Adraste, a rival, intrigues with Lyse, servant of Isabelle who has been spurned by Clindor, to unmask the secret lovers. The principals come together in a revelation scene in which Matamore runs off and Adraste is slain by Clindor. The latter is arrested on orders of Géronte, Isa-belle's father and partisan of Adraste's suit. Lyse undergoes a change of heart and intrigues with the jailer to have Clindor freed. The plot is successful and Clindor, Isabelle, Lyse, and the jailer flee. In a sudden change of circumstance Isabelle and Lyse are seen lamenting an apparent new infidelity by Clindor.

Though he succeeds in absolving himself before Isabelle for his attachment to one Rosine, the latter's husband's servants, led by one Eraste, slay him. The adventures of Clindor, begun in Act II and followed with attention by Pridamant and Alcandre, have apparently come to a sad end. But only apparently, for Alcandre restores the disconsolate father to good cheer with the revelation that the last few scenes were but those of a play, that Clindor, only playing the role of one Théagène, still lives, a member of an esteemed and lucrative profession. The play ends with the famous *éloge du théâtre*.

In the first version of the play, the play within a play terminates differently: having persuaded Isabelle of his fidelity, Clindor-Théagène attempts to dissuade Rosine from her passion for him. While doing so, he is slain by Eraste. Rosine, not Isabelle, then dies of remorse. Eraste then leads Isabelle off to be "comforted" by Florilame, Rosine's husband and Théagène's benefactor, who has long held her in secret affection.

3. Molière, *L'Impromptu de Versailles*

Molière has hurriedly assembled his troupe at the command of the king in order to put on a play in reply to Boursault's *Portrait du peintre,* a retort to Molière's *La Critique de L'Ecole des femmes,* in turn a *mise au point* of the criticisms more or less overtly directed at Molière's *L'Ecole des femmes.* To the troupe's complaint of being unprepared, Molière replies that the subject of the present play being a continuation of *La Critique,* the actors have only to continue in character from the earlier play and improvise. Roles are reassigned and the rehearsal is about to begin when the actors are interrupted by an annoying fop who brings more reports of the attacks on Molière. The fop shooed away, the rehearsal begins with Molière playing one of two ridiculous marquis who discuss the controversial dramatist, Molière. The two are joined by various others who attack Molière, while he is defended by one of the marquises. The inner play is broken off when one of the actors complains that Molière's counterattack is too tame, considering the personal nature of the attacks on him. He, however, defends the impersonal and professional character of his reply. The discussion is interrupted by the announcement that the king is ready to see the play he has been promised. Molière begs the king's indulgence to postpone that play, but promises to offer another in its stead. The messenger returns with the king's agreement and *L'Impromptu* concludes with the troupe preparing to offer the king another play.

4. Marivaux, *Les Acteurs de bonne foi*

Mme Amelin, aunt of Eraste, wishes to surprise Mme Argante, mother of Angélique, with a comedy in celebration of the engagement of Eraste and Angélique. Merlin, Eraste's valet, charged with the production, decides to put on an impromptu based on his own real affections for Lisette, *suivante* of Angélique, as well as on the real engagement to marry existing between Colette, the gardener's daughter, and Blaise, a peasant. The plot of the comedy is only to start from these relationships, for in the play Merlin and Colette are to fall in love. The players, playing themselves, begin rehearsals, but are unable to complete them because of the suspicions of Blaise and Lisette that the stage lovers "are only pretending to be pretending." The resultant confusion brings Mme Argante, who, upon being told of the cause of the ruckus, cancels the comedy. But Mme Amelin, vexed at the cancelation, decides to have her comedy anyhow, at Mme Argante's expense. Mme Amelin pretends to break her nephew's engagement to Angélique in favor of a young widow, Mme Araminte. To appease her guest and to make her change her mind once again, Mme Argante has Merlin play his comedy, but Blaise and Lisette are unable to continue this dangerous game. In all the confusion a notary arrives with a marriage contract which he asks Mme Argante to sign. She refuses to do so, thinking it for Eraste and Mme Araminte. Mme Amelin, satisfied at having had her little comedy, makes her friend see that the contract is the original one, just as Merlin and Colette convince their lovers that their pretense was only that.

5. Dumas, *Kean, ou Désordre et génie*

Eléna, the Countess de Koefeld, wife of the Danish ambassador to England, is warned against having an affair with the renegade actor, Kean, whose latest scrape involves the kidnaping of Anna

Damby, rich bourgeoise engaged against her will to Lord Mewill. Kean appears, having come to absolve himself of the abduction charges and to arrange a rendezvous with Eléna—both of which he accomplishes through a note she alone is permitted to read. At his private lodgings, Kean later receives Anna, who comes to the actor about advice about a possible stage career, now that she has broken her engagement. Kean discourages her because of the trials such a career entails. We next see Kean at an inn, where he is waiting to participate in the baptismal celebration for a child born to one of the *saltimbanque* associates of his early years. While there he meets Anna, who has been tricked into appearing at the inn through a false message in Kean's name. The author of the message is the masked Lord Mewill whom Kean accosts and unmasks in a famous tirade. We then see Kean at the Drury Lane Theater, where he is preparing to go on in the balcony scene from *Romeo and Juliet*. Eléna enters to keep her rendez-vous, but she is forced to flee at the approach of her husband and the Prince de Galles. The ambassador finds the fan Eléna inad-vertently drops in the dressing room and after a veiled threat to Kean leaves. The actor then pleads with the prince to give up his pursuit of Eléna for the sake of the actor's career. The prince is noncommittal and, after his departure, Kean discovers that the fan in question earlier had come from the prince. Kean feels un-able to go on as Romeo, but is persuaded to do so for the sake of his old friends. From the stage, Kean spies the prince in Eléna's box and is unable to continue with the scene. The next day the actor receives Anna who proffers her love and Eléna who with-draws hers. As the faithless mistress is about to leave, her husband arrives and she is forced to hide in another room. The ambassador is ready to duel with Kean, but a letter from the prince arrives in time to provide a plausible explanation of the presence of the fan in Kean's dressing room. The count leaves and the prince arrives in time to explain to Kean, who thinks Eléna has leaped from a window in her hiding place, that she has been rescued by means of a gondola below the window. The affair with Eléna over, Kean decides to accompany Anna to New York (where she hopes to make her career), thereby abiding by the temporary exile forced on him by the king for having insulted royal personages.

Notes

Chapter 1. The Drama. Ritual or Play? Pages 1–10.

1. Passim. See, in particular, Fergusson's appendix on the histrionic sensibility.

2. The translation of S. H. Butcher, *Aristotle's Theory of Poetry and Fine Arts, with a Critical Text and Translation of the Poetics*, 4th ed., p. 15.

3. Aristotle, *On the Art of Poetry a Revised Text with Critical Introduction, Translation, and Commentary*, ed. Ingram Bywater, p. 127.

4. *Homo ludens. A Study of the Play Element in Culture.* See especially ch. 1, "Nature and Significance of Play as a Cultural Phenomenon."

5. *The Oxford English Dictionary*, Vol. 1.

6. Henri Gouhier, *L'Essence du théâtre*, p. 13.

7. *Histoire du théâtre en France. Les mystères*, p. 390.

8. It is first according to F. S. Boas, "The Play within a Play," *A Series of Papers on Shakespeare and the Theater by Members of the Shakespeare Association*, p. 136.

9. Gustave Cohen, *Le Théâtre en France au moyen âge*, 1, 75.

10. I recognize with a recent critic that Fergusson's mirror image might lead to an inadequate view of certain works of literature: "For better or worse the analogy [of the work with the mirror] helped focus interest on the subject matter of a work and its models in reality, to the comparative neglect of the shaping influence of artistic convention, the inherent requirements of the single work of art, and the individuality of the author; it encouraged the striking of a dichotomy between those elements of the work which are demonstrably representative of the real world and those further verbal and imaginative elements said to be merely 'ornamental,' introduced to give pleasure to the reader; and it fostered a preoccupation with the 'truth' of art, or its correspondence, in some fashion, to the matters it is held to reflect." M. H. Abrams, *The Mirror and the Lamp. Romantic Theory and the Critical Tradition*, p. 34. I shall, myself, take exception to too literal a use of the mirror analogy in connection with Molière. However, I do not wish to throw out the baby with the bath water.

11. That is, the divine comedy gives way before the human comedy. *Comédie*, of course, not *pièce*, is the generic word for a play in this period of French letters. Now, inherent in the use of comédie in the more particular sense of "a play which is not a tragedy" was the notion, deriving from a medieval distinction, that a comedy not only dealt with private conditions and

everyday reality (the classical distinction as well) but also portrayed fictional events as opposed to the real—that is, historical—events of tragedy. We may wonder then if, as comédie came to assume the general sense of pièce de théâtre, the notion of fiction still inhered, thereby reflecting the general change of outlook I have been tracing here: the theater, tragic or comic, is an *art de plaire* as well as (if not primarily) an *art d'instruire*. And toward the end of the seventeenth century does comédie as a general word give way before pièce because of semantic confusion between the general use (which might designate a tragedy) and the particular use?

12. *Essais,* Bk. III, ch. 2, p. 779.

13. *Pensées,* ed. Louis Lafuma, *1,* 90.

14. "The Defense of the Illusion and the Creation of Myth," *English Institute Essays. 1948,* p. 76.

15. The play within a play has heretofore intrigued German scholars in particular. See, for example, Antonie Mersmann, *Das Schauspiel im Schauspiel im französischen Drama des XVII Jahrhunderts,* and Hans Schwab, *Das Schauspiel im Schauspiel zur zeit Shakespeares.* These two studies are limited by what might be called the triumph of illusion: concentrating on the inner play, the authors pay little attention to the relationship between it and the outer play which is, after all, itself an illusion. They take the primary play for reality itself, as it were. A more sophisticated and ambitious approach characterizes Joachim Voigt's *Das Spiel im Spiel. Versuch einer Formbestimmung an Beispielen aus dem deutschen, englischen, und spanischen Drama.*

Chapter 2. Shakespeare. The Play as Mirror. Pages 11–35.

1. *Deux Classiques français vus par un critique étranger. Corneille et son temps, Molière,* p. 484.

2. "The World of Hamlet," *Tragic Themes in Western Literature,* ed. Cleanth Brooks, p. 43.

3. For this chronology of the plays I have relied on the article by E. K. Chambers, "Shakespeare, William," *Encyclopedia Britannica,* Vol. 20.

4. "Manners, Morals, and the Novel," *The Liberal Imagination,* p. 207.

5. "Hamlet and His Problems," *Selected Essays.*

6. *Hamlet and Oedipus.*

7. *Shakespeare's Imagery and What It Tells Us.*

8. I have already alluded to the works by Fergusson, Fiedler, and Mack. For Speaight's interpretation of *Hamlet,* see his chapter on the play in *Nature in Shakespearean Tragedy.*

9. Aristotle, *Poetics,* trans. Butcher, p. 27.

10. *The Tragedy of Hamlet, Prince of Denmark,* Introduction, pp. xii–xiii.

11. "The Defense of the Illusion," p. 87.

12. *Nature in Shakespearean Tragedy,* p. 20.

13. *The Tragedy of Hamlet,* Introduction, pp. xiv–xv.

14. "The World of Hamlet," p. 55.

15. *Shakespeare,* p. 281.

16. "The Defense of the Illusion," p. 92.

17. Ibid., pp. 88–9.

Chapter 3. Rotrou. The Play as Miracle. Pages 36–46.

1. I have based this discussion of Marcelle on the scene from *Saint Genest* recently authenticated by Jacques Scherer in "Une Scène inédite de *Saint Genest*," *Revue d'histoire littéraire*, 50ème année (1950), No. 4, pp. 395–403.

2. See, for example, the objections of Hippolyte Parigot cited by Thomas Frederick Crane, ed., *Jean Rotrou's "Saint Genest" and "Venceslas,"* pp. 98–100.

3. *Port Royal, 1,* 169.

4. Kosta Loukovitch, *La Tragédie religieuse classique en France,* pp. 345–6.

5. Ernst Curtius has traced the world-stage metaphor from Plato to Hofmannsthal. He finds it dominant in only one Renaissance figure: Calderón. Yet the dominant conception of Calderón's most famous play is not that "life is a stage" but that "life is a dream"—a difference in conception with the significant implications I have drawn above. See Curtius, *European Literature and the Latin Middle Ages,* pp. 138–44.

Chapter 4. Corneille. The Play as Magic. Pages 47–61.

1. See M. Barras, *The Stage Controversy in France from Corneille to Rousseau.*

2. Pierre Corneille, *Oeuvres,* ed. Ch. Marty-Laveaux, 2, 430. The dates 1639–57 refer to the first edition of *L'Illusion comique.* Unless otherwise stated, all citations are based on Corneille's corrections after 1657. After 1660 the title was shortened to *L'Illusion.*

3. *Tragédie cornélienne, tragédie racinienne.* See, in particular, ch. 2, Pt. II, "La Surprise et la curiosité chez Corneille."

4. John C. Lapp has privately suggested to the author that the preceding analysis of Pridamant's role holds up only for the first viewing of *L'Illusion.* In subsequent viewings the spectator's identification with Pridamant is less complete, for dramatic curiosity is replaced by a kind of dramatic irony in which the spectator senses his superiority to Pridamant. Professor Lapp suggests that perhaps both relationships—identification and dissociation—obtain at once, this double perspective being characteristic of many of Corneille's plays.

5. *The Idea of a Theater,* p. 188.

6. *Le Sentiment de l'amour dans l'oeuvre de Pierre Corneille.* See, in particular, Pt. II, ch. 1, "Corneille et le théâtre autour de 1630."

7. See, for example, the pages on Corneille in Paul Bénichou, *Les Morales du grand siècle.*

8. *The Freedom of French Classicism,* p. 81 and passim.

9. Jean Rousset, *La Littérature de l'âge baroque en France,* and (limiting himself to the early Corneille) Imbrie Buffum, *Studies in the Baroque from Montaigne to Rotrou.*

10. Gonzague de Reynold, *Le Dix-septième Siècle,* p. 146.
11. Rousset, *La Littérature de l'âge baroque,* p. 213.
12. *In Search of Theater,* p. 386.

Chapter 5. Molière. The Play as Mask. Pages 62–75.

1. Ramon Fernandez, *La Vie de Molière,* p. 130.
2. Pierre Brisson, *Molière. Sa Vie dans ses oeuvres,* p. 99.
3. *Les Débuts de Molière,* p. 239.
4. *Deux Classiques français,* p. 316.
5. Ibid., p. 476.
6. *Molière. A New Criticism,* p. 36.
7. *Deux Classiques français,* p. 484.
8. *La Vie de Molière,* p. 42.
9. "Molière et la farce," *Revue de Paris,* 8ème année, *3* (1901), 135.
10. See, for example, Gustave Attinger, *L'Esprit de la commedia dell'arte dans le théâtre français,* and Léopold Lacour, *Molière acteur.*
11. See Molière, *Oeuvres,* ed. Eugène Despois and Paul Mesnard, *3,* 404–5, n. 3.
12. Michant, *Les Débuts,* p. 239.
13. Warren Ramsey, *Jules Laforgue and the Ironic Inheritance,* pp. 136–7.
14. *Molière,* p. 52.
15. Ibid., p. 42.
16. "De L'Essence du rire," *Oeuvres complètes,* p. 714.
17. Ibid.
18. "Les Comédies-ballets de Molière," *La Revue bleue* 6oème année (1922), pp. 40–2, 76–9.
19. *Journal, 1939–49,* p. 83.
20. *Pensées, I,* 156.
21. *La Vie de Molière,* p. 210.
22. *Journal, 1889–1939,* p. 658.

Chapter 6. Marivaux. The Play as Game. Pages 76–87.

1. See the introduction to the play by Jean Fournier and Maurice Bastide, eds., *Le Théâtre complet de Marivaux,* Vol. 2.
2. *Oeuvres complètes,* ed. J. Assezat, *8,* 368.
3. Attinger does discover in Marivaux's *joutes d'amour* the same atmosphere, if not the same degree of conventionality, as in the joutes d'amour of the commedia dell'arte, "a theater which made of these jousts its daily bread" (*L'Esprit de la commedia dell'arte dans le théâtre français,* p. 371). Attinger is the first, however, to minimize the importance of the Italians for a true understanding of Marivaux: "[Marivaux] is indeed the last writer whom one can reduce to the shafts and quips [of the old sketches], since, with him, it is the motives which count, and the hue of the passions" (p. 371) and ". . . even when we had reduced all these comedies to their frames, discovering there

love themes similar to those of the old sketches, we would not have proved much; for the art of Marivaux begins beyond" (p. 376).

4. *The Idea of a Theater*, p. 188.

Chapter 7. Legouvé, Dumas, and Sartre. Pages 88–114.

1. André Villiers, *La Psychologie de l'art dramatique*. See especially ch. 3, "La Fonction de l'acteur."

2. Charles Beaumont Wicks, *The Parisian Stage. Alphabetical Indexes of Plays and Authors*. Pt. I, *1800–15* and Pt. II, *1816–30*.

3. For these verses from *Le Cid*, the Marty-Laveaux edition gives as the definitive text "nourri," not "produit," in v. 1560 and "cessa," not "finit," in v. 1328.

4. Adapted from "Je t'en avais comblé, je t'en veux accabler" (*Cinna*, v.iii. 1708).

5. Adrienne actually begins her recitation earlier in Phèdre's speech, at "Juste ciel etc." (v. 839). In v. 851 Scribe and Legouvé have reinforced Adrienne's accusation by substituting "honteuse" for "tranquille."

6. The play by Dumas is a reworking of a manuscript created for the actor Frédérick Lemaître by Frédéric de Courcy and M. E. G. N. Théaulon de Saint Lambert. However, that the play as it now stands is more Dumas's than anyone else's is attested by the actor himself: the original manuscript "contained an idea well enough, but it essentially lacked that experience of the stage which consists of linking scenes in such a way that, following one upon the other, they succeed in giving not only interest but also life and passion to the drama" (*Souvenirs de Frédérick Lemaître*, p. 218). According to the actor, it was Dumas who provided that "experience of the stage."

7. ". . . literary romanticism of the nineteenth century responds to a psychological crisis in which the individual affirms himself as an individual, where the self, by a kind of liberation from activities long repressed, becomes fully conscious of himself and the external world now in exaltation, now in anguish," (Henri Berr, Avant-propos to Paul Van Tieghem, *Le Romantisme dans la littérature européenne*, p. xxv). Van Tieghem himself considers egomania as only one of a number of characteristics of romanticism (pp. 250 ff.). Abrams extracts as one of the seven crucial doctrines contained in Wordsworth's Preface to the *Lyrical Ballads* (extended Preface of 1802): "It is essential to poetry that its language be the spontaneous and genuine, not the contrived and simulated expression of the emotional state of the poet" (*The Mirror and the Lamp*, pp. 101–2). It is this lyricism which Kean brings into his art.

8. When presented in the winter of 1953, Sartre's adaptation was "en trois actes et sept tableaux" according to the program of the Théâtre Sarah Bernhardt. The text I have used, however, is in five acts and six tableaux: Alexandre Dumas, *Kean. Adaptation de Jean-Paul Sartre*.

9. Van Tieghem, *Le Romantisme*, p. 442.

10. *The Poetics*, Butcher's translation, p. 27.

11. Robert de Smet, *Le Théâtre romantique*, p. 98.

12. *La Psychologie de l'art dramatique*, p. 43.

13. "Lettre à M. d'Alembert," *Oeuvres complètes*, ed. V. D. Musset-Pathay, 2, 110.

14. Eugène de Mirecourt, *Les Contemporains. Frédérick Lemaître*, p. 55.

15. *Histoire de l'art dramatique*, 2, 250.

16. From *Lettres à Auguste Lewald*, quoted by Blaze de Bury, *Alexandre Dumas*, p. 121.

17. Préface to *Adrienne Lecouvreur* in *Comédies et dramas*, 2, 217 ff.

18. *The Opposing Self*, pp. 218–19.

19. Logan Pearsall Smith, *Words and Idioms*, p. 82.

Chapter 8. Schnitzler and Pirandello. Pages 115–133.

1. *The Playwright as Thinker*, p. 347.

2. Trans. Horace B. Samuel in *The Green Cockatoo and Other Plays*. I have used Mr. Samuel's translations throughout this chapter.

3. *The Playwright as Thinker*, p. 346.

4. *Feeling and Form*, p. 413.

5. *Naked Masks. Five Plays*, ed. Eric Bentley, pp. 364–5.

6. Ibid., pp. xvi–xviii.

7. *The Idea of a Theater*, p. 191.

8. *Le Théâtre de Luigi Pirandello*, p. 74.

9. *Naked Masks*, p. 372 (Bentley's trans.).

10. "Beauty, the splendour of truth, is a gracious presence when the imagination contemplates intensely the truth of its own being or the visible world, and the spirit which proceeds out of truth and beauty is the spirit of joy." From Joyce's essay on James Clarence Mangan, quoted by Herbert Gorman, *James Joyce*, p. 80.

Chapter 9. Anouilh. The Play as Maze. Pages 134–154.

1. *Jean Anouilh. Poet of Pierrot and Pantaloon*, pp. 90–1.

2. "Theatre in a Mirror," *Yale French Studies*, No. 14 (winter 1954–55), p. 63.

3. Ibid., p. 62.

4. *Jean Anouilh*, p. 162.

5. Ibid.

6. *Anouilh, Lenormand, Salacrou. Trois Dramaturges à la recherche de leur vérité*, p. 20.

Postface. Pages 155–157.

1. For the quickest confirmation of this impression see *Five Hundred Self-Portraits from Antique Times to the Present Day in Sculpture, Painting, Drawing, and Engraving*, ed. Ludwig Goldscheider, trans. J. Byam Shaw.

2. Lionel Trilling, who thus finds the basis for a comparison of Cervantes' great novel with *Madame Bovary*. See *The Liberal Imagination*, p. 211.

Bibliography

1. Plays

Anouilh, Jean. *L'Alouette*. Paris, La Table Ronde, 1953.
—— *Le Bal des voleurs, Léocadia,* and *Le Rendez-vous de Senlis,* Pièces roses. Paris, Calmann Lévy, 1945.
—— *Colombe, L'Invitation au château,* and *La Répétition, ou L'Amour puni,* Pièces brillantes. Paris, La Table Ronde, 1951.
—— *La Valse des toréadors.* Paris, La Table Ronde, 1952.
Calderón de la Barca, Don Pedro. *La Vida es sueño,* Comedias, Biblioteca de autores espanoles. Madrid, Rivadeneyra, 1848. Vol. 7.
Corneille, Pierre. *L'Illusion comique,* in *Oeuvres,* ed. Ch. Marty-Laveaux. Paris, Hachette, 1862. Vol. 2.
Desfontaines. *L'Illustre Comédien, ou Le Martyre de Sainct Genest.* Paris, Cardin Besongne, 1645.
Dumas, Alexandre. *Kean, ou Désordre et génie,* in *Théâtre complet.* Paris, Calmann Lévy, 1863–99. Vol. 5.
Gillet de la Tessonerie. *Le Triomphe des cinq passions.* Paris, Toussainct Quinet, 1642.
Gougenot. *La Comédie des comédiens,* in *Ancien Théâtre français,* ed. M. Viollet-le-Duc. Paris, Jannet, 1854–57. Vol. 9.
Kyd, Thomas. *The Spanish Tragedie,* in *The Works of Thomas Kyd,* ed. Frederick S. Boas. Oxford, Clarendon, 1901.
Legouvé, Ernest, and Scribe, Eugène. *Adrienne Lecouvreur,* in Legouvé's *Comédies et drames.* Paris, Ollendorff, 1888. Vol. 2.
Marivaux [Pierre-Carlet de Chamblain de]. *Les Acteurs de bonne foi,* in *Oeuvres complètes.* Paris, Duchesne, 1781. Vol. 2.
Medwall, Henry. *Fulgens and Lucres. A Fifteenth-Century Secular Play,* ed. F. S. Boas and A. W. Reed. Oxford, Clarendon, 1926.
Mercier, L. S. *Molière. Drame en cinq actes en prose, imité de Goldoni.* Amsterdam, et à Paris chez les libraires qui vendent les nouveautés, 1776.
Molière. *L'Impromptu de Versailles* and *Le Malade imaginaire,* in *Oeuvres,* ed. Eugène Despois and Paul Mesnard. Paris, Hachette, 1886. Vol. 3.
Pirandello, Luigi. *Ciascuno a suo modo.* 2d ed. Firenze, R. Bemporad, 1926.
—— *Così è (se vi pare).* Firenze, R. Bemporad, 1925.
—— *Naked Masks. Five Plays,* ed. Eric Bentley. New York, Dutton, 1952.
—— *Questa sera si recita a soggetto* and *Sei personnagi in cerca d'autore* (7th ed.). Milan and Rome, Mondadori, 1930.

Rotrou, Jean. *Le Véritable Saint Genest*, in *Jean Rotrou's "Saint Genest" and "Venceslas,"* ed. Thomas Frederick Crane. Boston, Ginn, 1907.

Sarment, Jean. *La Couronne de carton*, in *La Petite Illustration. Théâtre*, No. 346 (May 12, 1934).

Sartre, Jean-Paul. *Kean* (adaptation of Dumas's *Kean*). Paris, Gallimard, 1954.

Schnitzler, Arthur. *The Green Cockatoo and Other Plays*, trans. Horace B. Samuel. Chicago, McClurg, n.d.

Scudéry, Georges de. *La Comédie des comédiens*. Paris, Courbé, 1635.

Shakespeare, William. *As You Like It, Love's Labor Lost, The Merry Wives of Windsor, A Midsummer Night's Dream, The Taming of the Shrew, The Tempest*, and *The Tragedy of Hamlet, Prince of Denmark*, in *The Complete Works of Shakespeare*, ed. George Lyman Kittredge. Boston, Ginn, 1936.

———— *The Tragedy of Hamlet, Prince of Denmark*, ed. George Lyman Kittredge. Boston, Ginn, 1939.

Vega Carpio, Félix Lope de. *Lo Fingido Verdadero*, in *Obras*, published for the Real Academia Espanola. Madrid, Succesores de Rivadeneyra, 1894. Vol. *4*.

Wilder, Thornton. *Our Town*. New York, Coward-McCann, 1938.

———— *Pullman Car Hiawatha* in *The Long Christmas Dinner and Other Plays in One Act*. New York, Coward-McCann; New Haven, Yale University Press, 1931.

———— *The Skin of Our Teeth*. New York and London, Harper, 1942.

2. *Secondary Sources*

Abrams, M. H. *The Mirror and the Lamp. Romantic Theory and the Critical Tradition*. New York, Oxford University Press, 1953.

Aristotle. *Aristotle's Theory of Poetry and Fine Arts, with a Critical Text and Translation of the Poetics*, ed. and trans. S. H. Butcher. 4th ed. London, Macmillan, 1911.

———— *On the Art of Poetry. A Revised Text with Critical Introduction, Translation, and Commentary*, ed. Ingram Bywater. Oxford, Clarendon, 1909.

Attinger, Gustave. *L'Esprit de la commedia dell'arte dans le théâtre français*. Paris, Librairie Théâtrale, 1950.

Barras, M. *The Stage Controversy in France from Corneille to Rousseau*. New York, Institute of French Studies, 1933.

Bastide, Maurice, and Fournier, Jean, eds. *Le Théâtre complet de Marivaux*. Paris, Les Editions Nationales, 1947. Vol. 2.

Baudelaire, Charles. "De L'Essence du rire," *Oeuvres complètes*, ed. Y.-G. Le Dantec. Paris, Bibliothèque de la Pléiade, 1951.

Bénichou, Paul. *Les Morales du grand siècle*. Paris, Gallimard, 1948.

Bentley, Eric. *In Search of Theater*. New York, Knopf, 1953.

———— *The Playwright as Thinker*. New York, Reynal & Hitchcock, 1946.

Blaze de Bury, H. *Alexandre Dumas. Sa Vie, son temps, son oeuvre.* Paris, Calmann Lévy, 1885.

Boas, Frederick S. "The Play within a Play," *A Series of Papers on Shakespeare and the Theater by Members of the Shakespeare Association.* London, Oxford University Press, 1927. Pp. 134–56.

Borgerhoff, E. B. O. *The Freedom of French Classicism.* Princeton University Press, 1950.

Brisson, Pierre. *Molière. Sa Vie dans ses oeuvres.* Paris, Gallimard, 1942.

Buffum, Imbrie. *Studies in the Baroque from Montaigne to Rotrou.* New Haven, Yale University Press, 1957.

Chambers, E. K. "Shakespeare, William," *Encyclopedia Britannica.* 14th ed. New York and Chicago, 1937.

Champigny, Robert. "Theater in a Mirror. Anouilh," *Yale French Studies,* No. 14 (winter 1954–55), pp. 57–64.

Cohen, Gustave. *Le Théâtre en France au moyen âge.* 2 vols. Paris, Rieder, 1931.

Curtius, Ernst Robert. *European Literature and the Latin Middle Ages,* trans. Willard Trask. New York, Pantheon, 1953.

Diderot [Denis]. *Paradoxe sur le comédien,* in *Oeuvres complètes,* ed. J. Assezat. 20 vols. Paris, Garnier, 1875.

Eliot, T. S. "Hamlet and His Problems," *Selected Essays.* New York, Harcourt, Brace, 1950.

Fergusson, Francis. *The Idea of a Theater.* Princeton University Press, 1949.

Fernandez, Ramon. *La Vie de Molière.* Paris, Gallimard, 1929.

Fiedler, Leslie. "The Defense of the Illusion and the Creation of Myth," *English Institute Essays. 1948.* New York, Columbia University Press, 1949. Pp. 74–94.

Gautier, Théophile. *Histoire de l'art dramatique en France depuis vingt-cinq ans.* 6 vols. Leipzig, Edition Hetzel, Alphonse Durr, 1858–59.

Gide, André. *Journal, 1899–1939.* Paris, Bibliothèque de la Pléiade, 1948.

———— *Journal, 1939–49, et souvenirs.* Paris, Bibliothèque de la Pléiade, 1954.

Goldscheider, Ludwig, ed. *Five Hundred Self-Portraits from Antique Times to the Present Day in Sculpture, Painting, Drawing, and Engraving,* trans. J. Byam Shaw. Vienna, Phaidon, 1937; London, Allen & Unwin, 1937.

Gorman, Herbert. *James Joyce.* New York, Rinehart, 1948.

Gouhier, Henri. *L'Essence du théâtre.* Paris, Plon, 1943.

Huizinga, J. *Homo ludens. A Study of the Play Element in Culture,* trans. R. F. C. Hull. New York, Roy, 1950.

Jones, Ernest. *Hamlet and Oedipus.* London, Gollancz, 1949.

Lacour, Léopold. *Molière acteur.* Paris, F. Alcan, 1928.

Langer, Susanne K. *Feeling and Form.* New York, Scribner's, 1953.

Lanson, Gustave. "Molière et la farce," *Revue de Paris,* 8ème année, 3 (1901), 129–53.

Le Breton, André. "Les Comédies-ballets de Molière," *La Revue bleue,* 60ème année (1922), 40–2, 76–9.

Lemaître, Frédérick. *Souvenirs.* Paris, Ollendorff, 1880.

Loukovitch, Kosta. *La Tragédie religieuse classique en France.* Paris, Droz, 1933.

Mack, Maynard. "The World of Hamlet," *Tragic Themes in Western Literature,* ed. Cleanth Brooks. New Haven, Yale University Press, 1955. Pp. 30–58.

Marsh, Edward Owen. *Jean Anouilh. Poet of Pierrot and Pantaloon.* London, W. H. Allen, 1953.

May, Georges. *Tragédie cornélienne, tragédie racinienne,* Illinois Studies in Language and Literature, *32,* No. 4. Urbana, University of Illinois Press, 1948.

Mersmann, Antonie. *Das Schauspiel im Schauspiel im französischen Drama des XVII Jahrhunderts.* Munster, Druck der Westfalischen Vereinsdruckerei vorm. Coppenrathschen Buchdruckerei, 1925.

Michaut, G. *Les Débuts de Molière.* Paris, Hachette, 1923.

Mirecourt, Eugène de. *Les Contemporains. Frédérick Lemaître.* Paris, Havard, 1855.

Montaigne, Michel de. *Les Essais,* ed. Albert Thibaudet. Paris, Bibliothèque de la Pléiade, 1939.

Moore, W. G. *Molière. A New Criticism.* Oxford, Clarendon, 1949.

Murray, James A. H., Bradley, Henry, Craigie, W. A., and Onions, C. T., eds. *The Oxford English Dictionary.* 12 vols. plus supplement. Oxford, Clarendon, 1933.

Nadal, Octave. *Le Sentiment de l'amour dans l'oeuvre de Pierre Corneille.* Paris, Gallimard, 1948.

Nelson, Robert J. "Art and Salvation in Rotrou's *Le Véritable Saint Genest,"* French Review, *30* (1957), 451–8.

—— "*L'Impromptu de Versailles* Reconsidered," French Studies, *11* (1957), 305–14.

—— "Pierre Corneille's *L'Illusion comique.* The Play as Magic," PMLA, *71* (1956), 1127–40.

—— *The Play within a Play in French Dramatic Literature. Different Conceptions of the Theater Defined through the Study of a Dramatic Technique.* Unpub. diss., Columbia University, 1955.

Paolannacci, J.-Th. *Le Théâtre de Luigi Pirandello.* Paris, Nouvelles Editions Latines, 1951.

Pascal [Blaise de]. *Pensées,* ed. Louis Lafuma. 2 vols. Paris, Delmas, 1947.

Petit de Julleville, Louis. *Histoire de théâtre en France.* 2 vols. Paris, Hachette, 1880. Vol. *1, Les Mysteres.*

Radine, Serge. *Anouilh, Lenormand, Salacrou. Trois Dramaturges à la recherche de leur vérité.* Geneva, Edition des Trois Collines, 1951.

Ramsey, Warren. *Jules Laforgue and the Ironic Inheritance.* New York, Oxford University Press, 1953.

Reynold, Gonzague de. *Le Dix-septieme Siècle. Le Classique et le baroque.* Montreal, Editions de l'Arbre, 1944.

Rousseau, J.-J. "Lettre à M. d'Alembert," Oeuvres complètes, ed. V. D. Musset-Pathay. Paris, Dupont, 1824. Vol. 2.

Rousset, Jean. *La Littérature de l'âge baroque en France. Circe et le Paon.* Paris, J. Corti, 1953.

Sainte-Beuve, C.-A. *Port Royal.* 4th ed. Paris, Les Oeuvres Représentatives, 1929.

Sartre, Jean-Paul. "Qu'est-ce que la littérature?" *Situations II.* Paris, Gallimard, 1948.

Scherer, Jacques. "Une Scène inédite de *Saint Genest,*" *Revue d'histoire littéraire,* 50ème année (1950), No. 4, 395–403.

Schwab, Hans. *Das Schauspiel im Schauspiel zur Zeit Shakespeares.* Vienna and Leipzig, W. Braumuller, 1896.

Smet, Robert de. *Le Théâtre romantique.* Paris, Les Oeuvres Représentatives, 1929.

Smith, Logan Pearsall. *Words and Idioms.* London, Constable, 1948.

Speaight, Robert. *Nature in Shakespearean Tragedy.* London, Hollis & Carter, 1955.

Spencer, Theodore. *Shakespeare and the Nature of Man.* New York, Macmillan, 1942.

Spurgeon, Caroline F. E. *Shakespeare's Imagery and What It Tells Us.* New York, Macmillan, 1935.

Sypher, Wylie. *Four Stages of Renaissance Style.* New York, Anchor Books Original, 1955.

Trilling, Lionel. *The Liberal Imagination.* New York, Viking, 1950.

—— *The Opposing Self.* New York, Viking, 1955.

Van Doren, Mark. *Shakespeare.* New York, Holt, 1939.

Van Tieghem, Paul. *Le Romantisme dans la littérature européenne,* Vol. 76 in L'Evolution de l'humanité, ed. Henri Berr. Paris, Albin Michel, 1948.

Vedel, Valdemar. *Deux Classiques français vus par un critique étranger. Corneille et son temps, Molière,* trans. from the Danish by Mme. E. Cornel. Paris, Champion, 1935.

Villiers, André. *La Psychologie de l'art dramatique.* Paris, Colin, 1951.

Voigt, Joachim. *Das Spiel im Spiel. Versuch einer Formbestimmung an Beispielen aus dem deutschen, englishen, und spanischen Drama.* Unpub. diss., University of Göttingen, 1954.

Wicks, Charles Beaumont. *The Parisian Stage. Alphabetical Indexes of Plays and Authors.* Pt. I, *1800–15* and Pt. II, *1816–30.* University of Alabama Press, 1950 and 1953.

Wilson, J. Dover. *What Happens in "Hamlet."* New York, Macmillan, 1935.

Index

Real persons, to distinguish them from fictional characters, appear in capital letters. Italic page numbers signify a major discussion of the subject.

Yale Romanic Studies: *Second Series*